MADMAN IN A BOX

THE SOCIAL HISTORY OF *DOCTOR WHO*

MADMAN IN A BOX

THE SOCIAL HISTORY OF *DOCTOR WHO*

David Johnson

First published in the UK in 2016 by
Telos Publishing Ltd
5A Church Road, Shortlands, Bromley, Kent, BR2 0HP

www.telos.co.uk

Telos Publishing Ltd values feedback. Please e-mail us with any comments you may have about this book to:
feedback@telos.co.uk

Madman in a Box: The Social History of Doctor Who
© 2016 David Johnson
Cover Art © Iain Robertson

ISBN: 978-1-84583-939-0

The moral right of the author has been asserted.

British Library Cataloguing in Publication Data.
A catalogue record for this book is available from the British Library.

This book is sold subject to the condition that it shall not by way of trade or otherwise, be lent, resold, hired out or otherwise circulated without the publisher's prior written consent in any form of binding or cover other than that in which it is published and without a similar condition including this condition being imposed on the subsequent purchaser.

For Suzanne, who inspired me as a young man,

for Talia, who has loved and supported me through all my efforts,

for Dr Sackett, Dr Jiminez and Dr Hill, who inspired me as an adult, and

for Jessica and William, who remind me what is really important.

CONTENTS

Introduction	9
Computers	17
Life, Death and Technology	45
Scientists and their Gadgets	63
Evil and War	83
The Future of Humanity	105
Gender, Science and Society	117
Media and *Doctor Who*	141
Conclusion	161
Bibliography	163
About the Author	173

DAVID JOHNSON

Introduction

Many television programmes are remarkable, but few are truly unique in the proper sense of the word; a condition of having no equivalent. *Doctor Who* is certainly remarkable. It is remarkable for the highly innovative nature of its premise, in which a veteran traveller and a bevy of companions explore the entirety of space and time through the use of a technology-wrapped 'magic box' known as the TARDIS. One week the Doctor can be facing off against a medieval king, and the next battling an alien menace ten thousand years in the future, invariably saving the day and generally making things right with the universe. That sort of adventuring is certainly remarkable, but it is not unique. Other television programmes have travelled similar territory, both in time and in space. *Doctor Who* is remarkable for the passion its fans have for it, which a visit to a *Doctor Who* convention, or to the *Doctor Who Experience* in Cardiff, can attest to. Fans spend money, sometimes quite a lot of money, to reproduce the outfits of their favourite characters, collect the latest *Doctor Who* merchandise, or even construct elaborate reproductions of props, sets and gadgets. However, this is familiar territory, ground explored by many other television programmes and films, such as *Star Trek* and *Star Wars*. *Doctor Who* is remarkable for how prominently it has featured in the past several years of the BBC's annual reports, where it has been referred to as one of the biggest brands in their catalogue, playing in over 200 territories globally. Other significant brands are just as notably featured, though, such as *Strictly Come Dancing* (*Dancing with*

INTRODUCTION

the Stars in the US) and *Sherlock*.¹ The 2013/2014 BBC report also notes that 2013 was the fiftieth anniversary of *Doctor Who*.² This is remarkable, but it is not unique. Other programmes have had long runs, including *Come Dancing* (since 1949), *Blue Peter* (1958), *Coronation Street* (1960) and, in the US, *General Hospital* (1963).³ *Doctor Who* is clearly remarkable. But it is also genuinely unique, due to the combination of its different aspects: it is the longest-running globally-distributed science fiction television programme in history.

Other programmes and films have made forays into the field of science fiction for short visits, some of them roughly contemporaneous with the starting point of *Doctor Who*. *Star Trek* had its broadcast premiere in 1966, but lasted for only three series in its initial run. *The Twilight Zone*, *Lost in Space* and *The Time Tunnel* all ran in roughly the same period that *Doctor Who* premiered, but like *Star Trek*, lasted only a few series. Every one of these, in some capacity or other, has explored themes common in the genre of science fiction: renegade computers, the role of war, the nature of evil and, of course, time travel. But each and every one, because of its limited run, provides no more than a snapshot of these elements as they were perceived at the date of broadcast. Certainly *Star Trek* was prescient for the 1960s, predicting many key future technologies, including floppy discs, voice-controlled computers, communicators-cum-mobile phones and so on. But *Star Trek* as originally broadcast is indelibly a product of the late 1960s, complete with pastel colours, bikini-clad space women and gigantic computer systems replete with flashing lights and complex controls. Watching DVDs of the original series in the present time, one is

---

[1] *BBC Worldwide Annual Review 2012-2013*. (Kent: Cousin, 2013), 26.
[2] *BBC Annual Report and Accounts 2013/2014*. (London: British Broadcasting Corporation, 2014), p 2
[3] 'Long Runners.' *TVTropes.org*. Accessed 1 December 2013. http://tvtropes.org/pmwiki/pmwiki.php/Main/LongRunners

inevitably struck by how dated it can appear in terms both of the technology and of the social attitudes of its imagined future. The original *Star Trek* programme will always and forever be a time capsule of the 1960s, a fixed point in time.

Doctor Who features similar themes from the 1960s, certainly, but this is where it demonstrates how it is unique. Because it has been a television-broadcast entity for more than fifty years, it encompasses social attitudes, trends and ideas from 1963 right up to today, allowing viewers from the present to look back through history and understand how society itself has changed. In effect, *Doctor Who*, the television programme about travelling through time, has itself become a time machine. Specifically, the time machine of *Doctor Who* shows society's shifting perceptions and attitudes toward many aspects of life in the later part of 20th and the early part of the 21st Centuries.

This particular time machine is a bit overwhelming, though, given the programme's prolific nature. There have been 260 stories broadcast between 'An Unearthly Child' on 23 November 1963 and 'The Husbands of River Song' on 25 December 2015, with many of those, especially from the 1960s through the 1980s, made up of multiple episodes. Consequently there is a tremendous amount of data to process in this journey through time and space.[4] Based on average episode lengths, the total possible viewing time for *Doctor Who* works out at something over 400 hours, or over two weeks of viewing 24 hours a day. Even allowing for the loss of some of the early serials due to an unfortunate purge of the BBC archives in the 1970s, that is a tremendous amount of material to consider in a discussion of how *Doctor Who* shows changes in social attitudes and ideas over the past fifty years.

As such, a degree of selectivity is necessary. Therefore this

---

[4] The method to calculate the 260 story figure involves summing up early stories that had individual episode titles under the serial umbrella they are usually referred to by, and also counting as one story the two-episode serials in the revived programme. The figure also allows for both the twentieth anniversary story 'The Five Doctors', and the unbroadcast 'Shada' from Season Seventeen.

INTRODUCTION

discussion will focus on a specific selection of stories from both the 'classic' programme that ran from 1963 to 1989, with a TV movie in 1996, and the 'revived' programme that began in 2005 and may well run to 2063 and beyond. The stories discussed herein were selected not because they are the 'best' or favourite ones, but because they allow the most direct consideration of specific aspects of social attitudes from a particular time period. Admittedly, some of the stories, such as 'The Tomb of the Cybermen' and 'Genesis of the Daleks', rank as remarkably popular to this day. Others, such as 'Four to Doomsday' and '42', may not rank among the best, or even the good *Doctor Who* stories, but allow a consideration of specific themes or tropes within the genre of science fiction and the way people viewed social problems, technologies or issues of a given era.

It may be overzealous to consider portions of the 20th or 21st Centuries as 'eras', but at least on one level the term is reasonably apt. By way of comparison, for all the growth and development that characterised the Victorian world, there was a striking consistency of expectation, wage, social standing and the like. Granted, the 19th Century featured the rise of industrial capacity and many new technologies. Indeed, many core technologies of the 20th Century had their origins in the Victorian era or earlier, including the factory system, practical applications of electrical power and even the notion of mechanical computation as a forerunner of the modern computer. For all the progress, though, the world of 1830 was not markedly different from the world of 1890, beyond certain changes in fashion and a few innovative devices that were slowly percolating through society. The same could not be said of the 20th Century. The 20th Century, more than any other period in history, was a time driven by science and technology. The way developments of one aspect of 20th Century life impacted on other diverse aspects, from gender roles to morality to medicine, resulted in more rapid change that at any other time in human history.

Many events contributed to this rapid pace of change. Certainly two global wars and the radical progress they entailed helped things along. Events such as the development of powered flight in the first years of the century, and the incredibly large-scale industrial output of 'total war' for the First World War, left an indelible mark on the world, as well as providing the base from which the devastating destruction of the Second World War was possible. The jet-powered, nuclearised, computer-driven world created in the wake of the Second World War changed ever more quickly. Against this background of frenetic change, using the word 'era' to describe a relatively short span of time is probably fair. The era of the 1960s still lives in public memory as something distinct from the 1970s, and the 1980s again stands as something entirely different from the previous two decades. These time periods are distinct eras, even if it would be incorrect to assert that they are rigidly calendar-based. That is to say, that which the public mind holds to be the 1970s may not have begun precisely on 1 January 1970, nor is it the same starting date for every issue commonly associated with the 1970s (i.e. the feminism of the 1970s may have a different set of dates associated with it than the computer revolution of the 1970s) – but the premise of distinct social and technological eras for the later part of the 20th Century is a viable means of considering the time period and the changes it embodied.

Due to its longevity and wide-ranging stories, *Doctor Who* provides a way to explore and evaluate many different themes that run through the past fifty years of social history. It is worth noting that there is a well-established historical method of considering any work of art or media as a manifestation of the time in which it was created, just as the original *Star Trek* is irrevocably connected with the aesthetics of the late 1960s. This goes beyond a discussion centred on *Doctor Who*, but there is a field of history to draw from when considering a piece of media in its timeframe.[5] Suffice it to say, it is safe to place the different

---

[5] Curious readers may wish to explore writings by Theodor Adorno or Siegfried Kracauer as a means to explore the academic context for the historical methodology this book draws from.

INTRODUCTION

serials of *Doctor Who* in that same academic context, as representative samples of the time in which they were created.

Two cautions are necessary, though. The first is that obviously *Doctor Who* is not the only surviving document of the period. It is best to bear in mind that while *Doctor Who* offers a potential window for the armchair time-traveller to observe the past, it is not the only window, and of necessity this discussion will not be able to explore every possible aspect of the social and technological history for every theme. The reader is left to his or her own devices to explore a topic further, just as the Doctor would, driven by an innate sense of curiosity. The second caution is that the writers of *Doctor Who* stories may or may not have been deliberately trying to invoke themes or images prevalent at the time those stories were written. A certain amount of careful speculation is possible, but the degree to which specific characters or events can or should be directly equated to specific real-world counterparts is necessarily limited. Seldom have the writers of *Doctor Who* offered a Yertle the Turtle moment, as when Theodor Geisel (Dr Seuss) directly and bluntly connected Yertle the Turtle to Adolf Hitler.[6] Therefore it is important not to read too much into a specific aspect of the programme. For example, it is tempting to draw connections between the Daleks and the Nazis, especially in light of the later episodes' references to genetic purity and similar topics, but it is unlikely their creator Terry Nation ever had that idea in mind while drafting their first script in 1963.[7] The strongest arguments are to be found where recurrent themes or ideas of a very similar nature occur across the run of the series, as the way those ideas develop and are presented on the screen offers the least ambiguous means of assessing a general populist perception of them.

---

[6] Cynthia Gorney. 'Dr Seuss at 75: Grinch, Cat in Hat, Wocket and Generations of Kids in His Pocket.' *The Washington Post* (Washington, DC.) 21 May 1979.

[7] Terry Nation in discussions with the author, 1989 and 1990, at small conventions on the West Coast of the US.

To that end, this work explores a range of frequently-revisited themes over the course of more than fifty years of *Doctor Who*. Certainly the uses and perceptions of computers played a major role as the programme developed. Themes of war and the morality questions wars can raise manifest themselves in a wide range of serials, as do the ideas of medicine, death and immortality. The role of scientists and the general expectation of what science can do also frequently appear in *Doctor Who* serials, along with a host of gadgets and gizmos from the lab. Frequently *Doctor Who* allows viewers to consider the range of human potential with the help of science and technology, and to explore questions about gender roles over time. *Doctor Who* also serves as a way to evaluate the evolution of its own medium, television, as both the production and audience experience have changed substantially since the 1960s.

The unique television programme *Doctor Who*, the origins of which were dramatised as part of its fiftieth anniversary celebrations in the BBC production *An Adventure in Time and Space*, has in and of itself become an adventure in time and space. The 'madman with a box' has spent more than fifty years in a box, a television box, helping humanity explore social issues and new technologies in a safe and enjoyable way.

DAVID JOHNSON

Computers

Computer technology is ubiquitous in the world today, from clearly computer-like devices such as laptops and tablets to quite ordinary devices like programmable coffee machines and electronic door locks. The pervasion of computer technology into every aspect of daily life happened quickly, but certainly not overnight in either a literal or a metaphorical way. There was a steady progression from the 'electronic brains' of the 1950s and 1960s to the profusion of computerised bits everywhere in the world today. Part of this progression was technological, certainly, but equally important was a social component, in which western civilisation had to come to terms with what a computer was and what it could do. Popular media, such as *Doctor Who*, provided a safe means for society to evaluate the rise of the computer and play out some common 'what if?' scenarios as a means to grow comfortable enough with computer technology to embrace it fully. These same 'what if?' scenarios provided cautionary tales as well, and continue to do so in the present day. Through the presentation of the changing expectations of computers and the risks they could pose, *Doctor Who* demonstrates how society has adapted to the development and deployment of computer technology over the past fifty years.

Computers, readily defined as devices capable of performing calculations, pre-date *Doctor Who* by a very long time. A history of the development of computer technology could easily fill an entire volume, if not several. However, there are three crucial events in the history of computing that took place prior to the 23 November 1963 launch of *Doctor Who*, that defined the societal expectations of what a computer should look and act like, and these three events shaped the trope of the computer in *Doctor Who* through the 1970s. Particularly, the three events were the development of the theory of mechanical computing by Charles Babbage; the invention of electronic computing devices in the 1940s; and the 1952 Presidential election in the US. Each of these events provided a key component that shaped the image of the 'electronic brain' computers that dominated the first decade of *Doctor Who*'s run.

In a loose sense, mechanical computers have been around since the abacus. A gear-driven, single function computational device was developed by Blaise Pascal during the 17th Century. But it was Charles Babbage, in the 1830s, who really developed the core of what we recognise today as a computing machine. Driven by a desire to eliminate the errors that invariably appeared in the mathematical reference books of the early 19th Century, Babbage set out to design a machine that could not just compute complex maths but also output the results directly, eliminating the prospect for error. While a small section of a prototype was the only device Babbage ever constructed, he developed the central tenets of computing that are still used today, such as having a central unit to process the computation, a 'store' or memory section to hold information, and a unit to provide output of the finished result.[8] Babbage received additional support from Lady Ada Lovelace, who used her influence to promote the potential of the machine but more importantly developed ways to program it, effectively initiating the concept of software as distinct from the physical hardware Babbage designed. These core concepts still drive the operations of computers in the 21st Century.

Unfortunately, the Victorian world wasn't quite ready for the technology that Babbage and Lovelace pioneered, and so the idea languished for most of a century, steampunk machinations aside. One of the biggest problems in Babbage's design was that

---

[8] *The Machine That Changed the World*: 'Giant Brains.' Directed by John Palfreman. (1992, PBS). YouTube video https://www.youtube.com/watch?v=kYFRdV1r4nU

it worked with the ten digit decimal system that is the basis of everyday maths today. While easy for humans to process, this meant using a large number of gears and wheels both to run the computations and to produce the output, making the system cumbersome and slow. If there were some other, simpler way to represent the number required for mathematics, it might be possible to build a faster and simpler machine. The solution was a maths system commonly known as binary, in which each digit can be only a one or a zero, instead of the ten digits in the decimal system. Since each digit was limited to only two possibilities, it could be represented by a switch that was either on or off.

In the 1940s, a way to apply that binary system to maths was developed independently in three different places. Credit is certainly due to Konrad Zuse, who in 1941 in Germany assembled a binary maths circuit using electromechanical relays, as arguably this was the first application of electronic power to computational maths.[9] Credit is also due to technicians at Bletchley Park. Led by Thomas H Flowers with substantial input from Alan Turing, the Colossus project was developed to help crack Nazi encryption codes.[10] The machine used electronic logic to analyse the codes for patterns and exceptions, and was quite effective. However, it was also such a top-secret project that the public would not learn of it until it was declassified in the 1970s.[11] Because of the wartime secrecy of these two pioneering efforts, the machine that popularly got the credit as the first computer, and also defined the trope of computers in media for a generation, was the ENIAC, or the Electronic Numerical Integrator and Computer.

---

[9] 'Timeline of Computer History: 1941.' *Computer History Museum*, 2006, accessed 26 November 2013. computerhistory.org/timeline/year=1941

[10] Jack Copeland, 'Colossus: The First Large Scale Electronic Computer.' *colosuss-computer.com*, 2001, accessed 5 April 2015. http://www.colossus-computer.com/index.htm

[11] 'Breaking the Code.' *Computer History Museum*. 2015, accessed 5 April 2015. http://www.computerhistory.org/revolution/birth-of-the-computer/4/82

Funded by the US Army to help compute firing tables for artillery pieces, ENIAC was developed by Presper Eckert and John Mauchly using 19,000 vacuum tubes that could perform the maths required.[12] The war ended before ENIAC could be completed, but when it finally did make its public debut, Eckert and Mauchly made sure the footage of ENIAC in action was worth watching. They knew there was not much to see in terms of the actual work a computer does. Vacuum tubes, and later transistors and silicon chips, switch current on and off at blazingly fast speed, and at the end, some result appears on a screen or a piece of paper, but that does not make for compelling images. So, for the public performance of ENIAC, the designers developed and installed a special display unit fitted out with ping-pong ball halves with little lights inside them, so that it would look like the computer was doing something while it was working. From that day forward, every computer was expected to have lots of little blinking lights on it to show how powerful it was. Further, it was clear from the newsreel footage that ENAIC was simply massive, a room-sized machine that took an army of technicians to operate, and could 'add up a column of figures a yard long in a second.'[13] While its future uses were uncertain after it finished the tasks the US Army was using it for, it seemed possible that such a machine could be applied to a wide range of purposes, such as checking taxes or statistical analysis.[14]

While ENIAC was a proof-of-concept for electronic computing, and a crucial second step in the history of computing as presented in *Doctor Who*, it was assuredly primitive, and its designers knew that. Almost immediately

---

[12] Mark Weik. 'The ENIAC Story.' *Ordnance*, January-February 1961 as reproduced at http://ftp.arl.mil/mike/comphist/eniac-story.html accessed 2 September 2014.

[13] *Movietone News* [undated, circa 1946].
Directed by Edmund Reek. (1946, 20th Century Fox) YouTube video http://m.youtube.com/watch?v=OSYpYFEwr4o accessed 2 September 2014.

[14] ibid

after it was completed, Eckert and Mauchly began work on a successor machine that was more powerful and flexible. This computer, eventually named UNIVAC, short for UNIVersal Automatic Computer, was truly programmable, drawing data from spools of magnetic tape, the image of which would manifest itself in countless on-screen computers afterwards. But the development of UNIVAC itself was just another step forward in computing power. The marketing coup that the Eckert-Mauchly Computer Company pulled off in 1952 is what marks UNIVAC as the third, arguably most significant piece of computing history, setting the stage for computers and society in *Doctor Who*.

The Eckert-Mauchly Computer Company installed a UNIVAC in the CBS studio for the live election coverage of the US Presidential election in 1952. The results were beyond any expectation. Early in the evening, a news broadcaster introduced the UNIVAC, then spoke to it using something that looked like a microphone, asking it for a prediction based on early returns.[15] The impact of this action in the trope of early computers is hard to overstate. Speech recognition was far beyond the capacity of the UNIVAC system. Even natural language input by keyboard was far beyond the UNIVAC, which instead relied on very basic computer codes to program it. But the public didn't know that, and it appeared to be realistic that a person could speak to a computer and expect to get a result. Through the 1970s, speech recognition of natural language was an expected means of interacting with computers on television.

Compelling as the idea of the speech-driven computer was, what cemented computing in the minds of the western world was what happened, or didn't happen, next. The news anchor asked for a prediction, but UNIVAC was oddly silent. This was not a fault of the machine, but a fault of the CBS news bureau.

---

[15] *The Machine That Changed the World*: 'Inventing the Future.' Directed by John Palfreman. (1992, PBS). YouTube video https://www.youtube.com/watch?v=GropWVbj9wA

COMPUTERS

Polls had indicated all along that this election between Dwight D Eisenhower and Adlai Stevenson was going to be very close, probably too close to call until much of the tally had been recorded. However, when the UNIVAC was given the early results, it had indeed made a prediction, indicating that Eisenhower would win by a substantial margin. CBS was unwilling to air that result, and so in response to the spoken request, the computer appeared to be silent. Only at the end of the night, right before signing off, did the network admit that not only had the UNIVAC made a prediction, but it was the correct prediction, as Eisenhower was indeed winning by a very large margin.[16] The computer had been right, and so the die was cast. In the public mind, computers with lots of flashing lights, spinning tape reels and armies of highly trained technicians to run them, could not only think, but think faster and better than humans.

Into this public image of what computer technology could do and should look like came the TARDIS, and the Doctor with it. In the first episode of *Doctor Who*, 'An Unearthly Child', the TARDIS control room was everything the society of 1963 expected the future to look like. It was gleaming-white, with a large and complex console at the centre of it that was covered in dials, knobs, switches and readouts. It was never stated that there was a computer buried in all that technology, but the console looked computerish in its overall design, and the fact that apparently only the Doctor, and to an extent his granddaughter Susan, could safely operate it, further supported the expectation that computerised technology could be operated only by highly trained individuals and was not suitable for the rest of the world. This hands-off perception was reinforced when unwelcome guest Ian got a nasty shock trying to open the TARDIS doors, before the Doctor forcibly whisked him, fellow intruder Barbara and Susan back to the Stone Age at the end of the episode.

After that first adventure at the dawn of time, computers regularly popped up in the first three series of *Doctor Who*, either

---

[16] ibid

as background props, as in various Dalek stories, or as a more central element, such as the Conscience computer for enforced justice in 'The Keys of Marinus'. However, late in the era of first Doctor actor William Hartnell, the final story of Season Three was 'The War Machines', featuring a very poignant evaluation of computer technology for viewers in 1966. The story originated from a conversation that story editor Gerry Davis had with Dr Kit Pedler, who had been consulted with a view to providing the programme with useful scientific background material. Part of the conversation involved cybernetics and systems of control, features of which would later be incorporated into the Cybermen. For 'The War Machines', Dr Pedler applied the idea of control and development in the context of an artificially intelligent computer, a machine truly capable of independent logic. Dr Pedler was not the first scientist or computer technician to consider this, as Alan Turing had proposed in the 1950s a means of evaluating whether or not a computer possessed some degree of intelligence, through the use of a 'Turing Test'. But what Dr Pedler added that made such a compelling story for *Doctor Who* was a way for that computer to connect with other systems around it.[17] In 1966, computer networking was meaningfully nonexistent. An experiment in 1965 had allowed two computers in the same lab to communicate data to one another, but the ARPANET, the grandfather of today's internet, would not begin its first efforts until 1969.[18] As the computer system in the serial was intended to interface with others all around the world, a nod

---

[17] David Banks. *Doctor Who: Cybermen*. (London: W H Allen & Co. 1990), 8. The Turing Test relied on a conversation taking place only by text message. If at the end of a prescribed period of time, usually listed as twenty minutes, the individual running the test could not say with certainty that the entity at the other end of the conversation was a computer, Alan Turning argued that such a computer must be said to have some measure of intelligence.
[18] Kim Ann Zimmerman. 'Internet History Timeline: From ARPANET to the World Wide Web'. *Live Science*. 4 June 2012. Accessed 14 January 2016. http://www.livescience.com/20727-internet-history.html

at least must go to the remarkably prescient Dr Pedler for developing a concept akin to the internet.

As remarkable as the underlying ideas from Dr Pedler were, the on-screen execution of those ideas highlights some significant perceptions of computers for the general public. The principal enemy of 'The War Machines' was the computer WOTAN, designed by one Professor Brett with full support from the British government. WOTAN was everything viewers in 1966 would expect a computer to be. It was room-sized, with large banks of intricate electronic equipment, replete with the flashing lights of the ENIAC and the tape reels of the UNIVAC. Perhaps most interesting in this design, though, is the fact that in several instances there are fairly close shots of the computer systems, showing what are purported to be display panels with lots of little indicator lights on them, yet the small lights never light up. Instead, it is obvious that behind the façade there are only three or four larger light bulbs flashing. This trivial detail is a telling manifestation of the public perception of what computers should be. Computers had flashing lights, and what those lights were for, if anything, was irrelevant.

The way WOTAN is operated and tested in the serial further emphasises the significant gap between the realities of computer technology in 1966 and the public expectations of it at that time. When the Doctor first encounters WOTAN, he is sceptical of its power, and verbally poses it a question, asking for the square root of a large number. WOTAN dutifully provides the print-out of a correct answer – although later in the serial it develops the ability to speak as well. But in the simple interaction between the Doctor and the computer, a fundamental public misunderstanding is laid bare. Any computer, even going back to Babbage's mechanical design, could do the maths required to compute a square root, and do it faster than any human could, at least for large numbers. But the majority of humans have problems with maths, especially complex maths. However, speaking is easy for most humans. Speaking generally requires little or no thought, as public figures often demonstrate.

The difference between the two processes, doing maths and using language, is at the heart of the gap between public expectations and computer realities. Codifying maths problems is straightforward, even for complex equations in a calculus system. Granted, in 1966 it probably took someone with highly developed mathematical skills to break down the processes into the binary or hexadecimal codes a computer could cope with, and to enter those codes in the correct order. But once the computer had the data input, coming up with a solution, even to complex orbital dynamics problems such as those facing early spaceflight engineers, was a job that took seconds, or at most minutes, as opposed to days or weeks of human brain time. The key to a successful computing outcome lay in the inputting of the data without any error – a fact spectacularly affirmed by the 1962 crash of the NASA rocket carrying Mariner 1, an early probe to Venus, due to a misplaced comma in the data.[19] For a human, a misplaced comma in a written construct might result in annoyance or at worst a bit of confusion, but human common sense can usually resolve this without blowing up a multimillion dollar rocket. However, as any user of Siri or other voice-to-text technology will tell you, even in 2016 just getting a computer to recognise normal speech patterns can be an uncertain prospect. Therein lies the gap in public perception. Since a computer can do something humans find difficult to do, such as maths, then surely it should also be able to do something humans find easy to do, such as understand spoken language. Buried in all this is a fundamental assumption that computers can think.

Doctor Who certainly reinforced that notion with the early serials. In episode one of 'The War Machines', Professor Brett asserts, 'WOTAN can not only think faster than Polly or myself, it can also type faster.' Polly, Brett's secretary and new companion to the Doctor, adds, 'And it never makes mistakes.' At a later press conference, a reporter asks Sir Charles, the

---

[19] 'Mariner 1' *NASA*, 2014, accessed 28 November 2013. http://nssdc.gsfc.nasa.gov/nmc/spacecraftDisplay.do?id=MARIN1

government representative for WOTAN, who has the power to control WOTAN. Sir Charles replies, 'No-one operates WOTAN. WOTAN operates itself ... [It] thinks logically, without any political or private ends.' Admittedly, the ability to compute maths very quickly is a form of 'thought', but what was not understood in 1966, and is still quite problematic in the 21st Century, is how to codify the day-to-day common sense even a five-year-old child has. As an example, a computer can easily store the birth dates of a million people, and access those nearly instantaneously when asked, but unless it is specifically programmed to do so, it will never occur to a computer to wish any of those million people 'Happy birthday'. Independent of the human operating it, the computer itself knows nothing of the significance of or customs behind birthdays.

But to the public mind in 1966, computers were intelligent, and the risk of computers outthinking humans seemed very real. WOTAN was the embodiment of this fear. This is an area where *Doctor Who* really excels as a means of evaluating social and technological changes. The 'what if?' scenario of 'The War Machines' is a familiar one now to anyone who consumes much science fiction media: what if the computers decided humans were no longer necessary? This is precisely what WOTAN does. Brett, firmly under the control of WOTAN due to its hypnotic power, says, 'We [humans] have failed. We cannot develop the world any further. WOTAN has decided the world cannot progress further with mankind running it.' At least for this serial, the humans are unwilling slaves to the computer, hypnotised or coerced into doing its bidding, as Brett has been. Security man Major Green puts this point quite succinctly when he says to Polly, in episode three, 'You are working for the machines. You are an instrument only. You have ... no will of your own.' Surely there had to be more than a few contemporary factory workers and even businessmen who felt much the same in their own day-to-day lives? However, in *Doctor Who*, humans do eventually fight back against WOTAN, as the Doctor sends a reprogrammed robotic War Machine to blast it at the end of episode four; a reassuring assertion that the mind could still triumph over the machine in the end.

A more frightening presentation of computer technology emerged in the Season Five story 'The Ice Warriors', with Patrick Troughton now playing the role of the second Doctor. In this serial, the Doctor and his companions Jamie and Victoria arrive at some unspecified future time on Earth, only to find a paralysing ice age gripping the planet. At a computer-controlled base, scientists and bureaucrats butt heads while trying to develop and refine an ioniser that will melt the ice. To complicate matters, buried in the ice just near the base is a spaceship crewed by members of one of the iconic *Doctor Who* monster races, the Ice Warriors, who decide to try to take control of the Earth. This particular serial is replete with messages about the role of science in society, ecological concerns and so on, but it also very prominently features a computer, this time not as an enemy directly, but as a limiting factor for the humans in the base. As with almost every other computer system in *Doctor Who* from 1963 through the 1970s, it is sited in a gleaming white room with lots of control panels covered in switches, dials and prominent flashing lights, and is controlled by spoken commands, thereby meeting the public expectation for the trope of a computer.

The 'what if?' scenario 'The Ice Warriors' plays out is akin to the theme of 'The War Machines', but in this case, the humans voluntarily subsume their will to the computer, instead of being coerced. The Doctor repeatedly offers ideas, only to have the humans, most notably the base controller Clent and the main technical advisor Miss Garrett, say they will check with the computer. Humans of the future seem to have given up the ability to use their own minds, instead saying, 'If you want an important decision, I'll ask the computer.' The Doctor provides an antithesis to this, stating that he uses computers, 'only when I have to'. As the story moves toward its climatic point, Clent says, 'We obey the computer', to which a renegade scientist named Penley replies, 'You're not a man. You're just a machine slave.' Miss Garrett then defends Clent, saying, 'Our trust is in the great computer.' Later, near the end of episode six, this tone becomes even more reverential, as Clent states, 'The computer is our supreme advisor', and Miss Garrett adds in a zealous voice, 'We must obey ... We trust the computer. It is our strength and our guide.'

The redemption for the story's humans comes when the computer is given all the data it requires to make a decision, and effectively shorts itself out as it cannot resolve two conditions that cancel out core elements of its own internal programming. As the crisis point nears, even Clent admits this, suggesting, 'Because [the computer is] so logical, it can't gamble. It can't take risks.' However, Clent also is unwilling to take risks, such a slave to the computer is he. It takes the renegade scientist Penley to come back and save the day with his assertion, 'This is a decision for a man to take, not a machine,' before running the ioniser to full power, destroying the Ice Warriors' ship in the process, despite the risk that this might also destroy the base. Perhaps ironically, though, as soon as the threat from the Ice Warriors is gone, Clent directs Miss Garrett to return ioniser control to the global computer system to coordinate the final assault on the encroaching glaciers, a task entailing timing too precise to rely on human control.

Through the 1960s in *Doctor Who*, the presentation of the computer is fairly standardised, with large banks of incomprehensible equipment, and skilled technicians running the machines (when then machines aren't running themselves), and with humans usually needed at the end to save the day. Yet, as at the end of 'The Ice Warriors', there is also a demonstration of the necessary role computers were increasingly assuming in society. To do menial tasks such as tallying bookkeeping sums, or to coordinate really precise actions, computers did play a valuable role. A highly visible application of this was on display in 1968 and 1969 when the US launched Apollo astronauts to the Moon, depending on the Apollo Guidance Computers (ACGs) of the command module to control key aspects of the flight while the ship was behind the

Moon and out of contact with the Earth.[20] At the time, the computer systems on board the Apollo spacecraft were the most powerful for their size that had ever been constructed, thanks in part to the rapid development of the integrated circuit, more commonly known as the computer chip. Because of the remarkable progress in computer chip design and manufacturing techniques, the room-sized or wall-sized computer system could be replaced by more affordable 'mini-computers' such as Data General Corporation's Nova, a mini-computer with four kilobytes (4K) of memory that went on sale in 1968 for $8,000, or about one-third the price of a home in the US at the time.[21]

While it was unlikely to find these mini-computers in domestic homes in 1968, or even in 1971, by 1972 that had begun to change. The year 1972, in addition to marking the premier of the video game Pong, also saw the advent of the HP35 digital calculator from Hewlett Packard; and while this commanded a premium price for the time period, it was the first actually useful, affordable home computer device.[22] A further development took place in 1972, although it would take some time to really change the world. Electronics company Intel began selling the 8008 microprocessor.[23] The microprocessor was the key to the future of computing, as it was a mass-

---

[20] 'Timeline of Computer History: 1968.'
Computer History Museum, 2006, accessed 2 January 2014. computerhistory.org/timeline/year=1968?
[21] 'Nova/Super Nova' sales brochure. (Southborough: Data General) (ND, before 1970) PDF as found at *Computer History Museum*, accessed 2 January 2014.
http://www.computerhistory.org/brochures/companies.php?alpha=d-f# and 'Median and Average Sales Prices of New Homes Sold in the US.' *US Census Bureau*, accessed 2 January 2014. http://www.census.gov/const/uspriceann.pdf
[22] 'Timeline of Computer History: 1972.'
Computer History Museum, 2006, accessed 2 January 2014. computerhistory.org/timeline/year=1972
[23] ibid

produced computing engine, whereas previous computers had been driven by custom-built and highly complex circuits. With the 8008 chip, and later others like it such as the Motorola 6502 and the Zilog Z80, an enthusiast could build a working computer at home. Granted, while the number of people building and using computers in 1972 was quite small, it was at least an order of magnitude higher than it had been in 1970, when mini-computers were still exclusively the province of universities and businesses with deep pockets.

This is one possible reason why a new element had to be introduced when Jon Pertwee's incarnation of the Doctor faced off against a computer adversary in 'The Green Death' in 1973. In the story, the principal foe is a computer known as the BOSS, the Bimorphic Organisational Systems Supervisor. The more visible problems of oversized maggots and toxic green sludge are found to be by-products of the BOSS's plan to promote maximum efficiency, productivity and profit; a plan that harks back to earlier automation fears of the 1960s. The BOSS is a substantial improvement over the Doctor's earlier computer foes, although he still describes it as little more than a 'gigantic adding machine'. But the BOSS is the first computer shown to be linked to a human brain, through a Global Chemicals executive referred to only as Stevens. Perhaps because of this, it is much more 'human' than previous computer enemies. It hums tunes and has a very human and well-inflected voice, even though the visual representation of the system is the same as that of any other computer shown prior to it, with a room full of databanks covered in flashing lights and complex controls. The most striking difference is that the story makes an open acknowledgement that computers and computer logic alone are unlikely to be much of a threat anytime soon. Instead, a much more direct link between computers and humans is necessary. Even the BOSS admits that although humans are inefficient, that inefficiency often leads to surprising progress. The BOSS says, 'I programmed Stevens to program me to be inefficient,' to be more like a human.

Arguably 'The Green Death' is the last of the classic 'sentient computer' stories in *Doctor Who*, inasmuch as the computer plays the principal enemy and is bent on taking over the world or enslaving humanity. Fourth Doctor actor Tom Baker's premiere story, 'Robot', does feature computers and a sentient robot wreaking havoc, but the robot is more of a *Doctor Who* take on the *King Kong* story than a commentary about computers. The most the Doctor will allow about computers themselves in 'Robot' is that they are just, 'very sophisticated idiots.' He adds that they, 'do exactly what you tell them to do at amazing speed, even if you order them to destroy you.' That simple statement illustrates a significant social shift in the perception of the computer; and the reason for the shift is not terribly hard to identify.

'Robot' played on BBC television in December 1974 and January 1975. In January 1974, with that month's issue of the periodical *Popular Mechanics,* the social perception of computers changed irrevocably with the announcement of the Altair.[24] The Altair was a build-at-home kit computer, but it was a mass-produced one. Rather than figure out how to design and construct it from scratch, buyers would get a set of circuit boards and parts that could be easily assembled by anyone with basic soldering skills. Success was immediate, and overwhelming. The company quite literally could not keep up with the number of orders. In fact, the reason Altair did not become a household name like Apple or IBM in the late 1970s and early 1980s is that it was so overwhelmed by its initial success that there was not enough manpower to develop planned accessories, such as larger memory boards and other peripherals. By the time Altair finally caught up enough with the computer kit orders, interest in the machine had already peaked as users moved on to other options. The Altair kit computer faded into relative obscurity – but not before demonstrating there was a ready market for personal computers.

---

[24] 'Timeline of Computer History: 1974.'
Computer History Museum, 2006, accessed 3 January 2014. computerhistory.org/timeline/year=1974

COMPUTERS

If the Altair demonstrated the interest in owning personal computers, it also demonstrated that those computers were unlikely to take over the world anytime soon. In fact, the spread of computers served only to highlight just how limited they actually were. At its most basic, the operation of the Altair was along the lines of turning it on and watching the little red bulb light up. Even the later, mass-produced computers of the 1970s, such as the Apple][and the Commode Pet, would do little more than display a blinking cursor when they turned on. This hardly seemed menacing, although it might have been frustrating when the computer frequently responded to a user's typing with a beep and '?Syntax Error'.

Considering the changes the personal computer brought with it, the Tom Baker era of *Doctor Who* can be seen as a transitional phase for the programme, moving away from evil computers to focus instead on robots and androids. While robots had featured prior to Tom Baker's run, which lasted from December 1974 to March 1981, his Doctor faced off against robotic foes no fewer than five times, and also brought into the TARDIS the first robotic companion, the redoubtable K-9. Arguably, a robot is little more than a computer encased in a mobile machine that can interact directly with the physical world; but in the late 1970s that physical interaction was much more interesting than raw computers. Mostly the stories about robots, such as 'The Robots of Death' and 'The Androids of Tara', featured human-looking androids and tried to confront questions of whether or not the robots were really under human control, and whether or not the programming within them could be trusted. Humans of 2016 still find themselves considering such questions – and others, such as whether or not a robot can do the job a human has done – so there is little room there to evaluate a change in attitude over time, despite the programme's longevity. While industrial robots are increasingly common in 2016, and even home robots such as the Roomba are available, proper artificially-intelligent robots akin to the Super-Voc in 'The Robots of Death' remain firmly in the realm of science fiction, despite dire warnings from Professor Stephen

Hawking. The unimpressive efforts at the DARPA Robots challenge for 2015 served as a firm reminder of how distinctly ability-challenged robots still are when confronted with a routine task such as opening a door.[25]

By the late 1970s, computers were no longer the stuff of science fiction, but increasingly common items in businesses and homes. More directly relevant for *Doctor Who*, none of the computers had tried to take over so much as a toaster, let alone the world. However, Tom Baker's version of the Doctor did feature two notable appearances by computers, in back-to back serials in December 1976 and January 1977. 'The Deadly Assassin' introduced the computer system known as the Matrix, the repository of Time Lord knowledge on Gallifrey. The follow-along serial 'The Face of Evil' introduced Xoanon, an artificial-intelligence computer that the Doctor unwitting made schizophrenic many years before the events of the story take place.

Of these two stories, 'The Deadly Assassin' offers more interesting considerations as far as social context is concerned. This is not to say that the notion of a schizophrenic computer isn't interesting, but 'The Face of Evil' offers little that is actually new, as the 1973 serial 'The Green Death' introduced the concept of a human/computer fusion, and Arthur Clarke's seminal *2001: A Space Odyssey* explored a computer with psychological problems in much greater depth. What 'The Deadly Assassin' introduces viewers to is an early application of virtual reality. In the story, the Doctor must link into the Matrix in order to find out who is really behind the assassination of the Time Lord President, a crime of which he himself is at first accused. Once inside, he encounters a world that seems to be physical in nature, replete with swamps and

---

[25] 'At DARPA Challenge, Robots (Slowly) Move Toward Better Disaster Recovery.' *NPR*, 7 June 2015, accessed 10 June 2015. http://www.npr.org/sections/alltechconsidered/2015/06/07/412533 020/at-darpa-challenge-robots-slowly-move-toward-better-disaster-recovery

attacking biplanes. At one point, after he is wounded, he attempts to assert his control over the system, saying 'I deny it!' to cause the wound to disappear. The real assassin, Chancellor Goth, already in the Matrix, reasserts his power, leaving the Doctor trapped in the virtual reality for a while longer.

There are several ways to consider this new aspect of computer technology in *Doctor Who*. After Pong in 1972, a few modestly successful video games had come to the market, including early efforts at first-person driving games, albeit that these were little more than blocky, symbolic representations of a roadway at night.[26] The public was therefore at least receptive to the idea of a computer-controlled world, even if the early worlds consisted only of simple repetitive images that were unlikely to be mistaken for reality. For future-minded thinkers, though, even in 1976 it was possible to conceive of a time when a computer could create a complete world that would immerse the player in life-like images. *Doctor Who* took this immersion to the next level, in which the computer-user himself was immersed in a world that was indistinguishable from reality, including the physical sensations of reality. Even in 2016, this is beyond the reach of current computer systems, although great strides have been made in the 21st Century. But more poignant than the possibility of a true virtual reality, and the question whether or not a virtual death could cause a real death in the outside world, the question *Doctor Who* allowed viewers to consider was: who would be in charge of such an experience? From a 21st Century perspective, such stories have become almost a trope unto themselves, as a plethora of holodeck stories in *Star Trek: The Next Generation*, the *Tron* films and *The Matrix* film series have all demonstrated. But *Doctor Who* afforded a first look at these considerations long before, even if the technology of early computers like the Altair was far removed from the ability to provide a virtual world.

If the Altair represented a first foray into personal

---

[26] Author experience from the 1970s and 1980s. Readers can experience the same games via phone/tablet apps such as Atari's Greatest Hits.

computing, later machines cemented the computer as a populist device. The first round of mass-produced computers such as the TRS-80 series, the Apple][and the IBM PC offered a great deal of potential power for users, but they were still costly, with even the most budget-minded TRS-80 starting at $599.95, or around £300.[27] Although far cheaper than earlier machines, this was still quite a bit of money to lay out for a computer that didn't do a whole lot. It would take something much more affordable to get computing power into the hands of the masses. Several offerings came about in the early 1980s, but perhaps the most groundbreaking machines were the Sinclair ZX80 and its successor, the ZX81. At £99.95 in 1980, the ZX80 was the first really affordable computer system offered. While its capabilities were limited, it gave a lot of people their first chance to get their hands on a 'real' computer, and so it sold fairly well, moving 50,000 units.[28] The ZX81, when it premiered in 1981, sold for only £69.95, and offered far more computing capacity, which may explain why it sold ten times as many units as the ZX80, although the start of the BBC Computer Literacy Project at the end of 1981 may also have helped drive interest.[29] With affordable computers for the masses and the rise of ready-made computer software packages, by 1982 the mystique of the computer had largely vanished from the public imagination, replaced by a tangible product that was in a great many homes and offices, a tool to get work done or play a game on, but hardly a threatening presence, save perhaps when it crashed just as a report was required. Humans were firmly in control of the ZX81, and the plethora of machines like it, and were used to interacting with a computer via a keyboard, a method still ubiquitous today, albeit with notable limitations

---

[27] 'Radio Shack TRS 80 (Model 1).' *oldcomputers.net*, 10 December 2013, accessed 2 January 2014. http://oldcomputers.net/trs80i.html
[28] 'Sinclair ZX80.' *oldcomputers.net*, 10 December 2013, accessed 2 January 2014. http://oldcomputers.net/trs80i.html
[29] 'ZX81: Small black box of computing desire.'
BBC News, 11 March 2011, accessed 2 January 2014. http://www.bbc.co.uk/news/magazine-12703674

COMPUTERS

Questions about human-computer interactions and the limitations of these are a crucial component of the serial 'Warriors of the Deep' from the era of fifth Doctor actor Peter Davison. In this, the year is specified as 2084, and the world is engaged in a heightened Cold War again. The unnamed enemy and the supposed 'good guys' have bases deep under the sea, stocked with nuclear missiles and ready to fire at a moment's notice. Central to the defence of the Sea Base that we see in the story is a computer system, not intelligent or even verbally interactive, but lightning-fast in its ability to execute commands. The key to the speed of this system is the so-called sync operator, a human who can directly sync his brain with the computer to give the best possible edge – presumably because, when a nuclear holocaust is imminent, even microseconds count. Admittedly, this piece of kit is largely just a backdrop to the central storyline, which features the return of third-Doctor-era monsters the Silurians and the Sea Devils in their own Cold War efforts against the human race, but it is nevertheless instructive.

The Sea Base harks back to the type of gleaming white super-structure found in William Hartnell and Patrick Troughton stories; the promise of a brighter, cleaner future. However, in 'Warriors of the Deep', the computer has become a tool instead of a central figure with great authority. Its presentation is still as a large box with lots of lights and buttons, but it also prominently features a keyboard. This mode of operation is echoed in the TARDIS redesign that premiered in the previous episode, the twentieth anniversary special 'The Five Doctors', whereby the control console is now covered in keyboards and monitors rather than the mysterious dials and indicators of all previous designs. But in both cases, a human (or Time Lord) operator is still integral to the system, which is incapable of acting without that input and control. Granted, from time to time, the Sea Base computer still relays an order from higher command centres to run simulations to fire the missiles, but it is not the computer itself that is making the decision. 'Warriors of the Deep' most directly shows the impact that the first wave of the computer revolution had on the public mindset. By the end of 1983, *Doctor Who* had caught up with the public perception of what a computer was, what it looked like and what it could do, and largely the population seemed to be content with the change, seeing the computer no longer as a malevolent bogeyman but instead as a tool to get things done. It is perhaps ironic, then, that the serial finished just days before a significant shift in computer technology debuted.

The final episode of 'Warriors of the Deep' aired on 13 January 1984. Human/computer interactions took an irrevocable turn again on 24 January 1984, when Apple introduced the first Macintosh computer, with its graphical user interface, or GUI. Admittedly, the Macintosh was not the first computer to have such an interface. Earlier computers, such as the STAR from the Xerox Palo Alto Research Centre (PARC) and Apple's own Lisa, had developed the idea of a point-and-click interface, and Microsoft's variant of the GUI, known as Windows, would come to dominate the computer industry for most of the 1990s and into the 21st Century. However, the Macintosh was arguably the catalyst that drove a fundamental shift in the way people interacted with computers, even if the fallout from this change would not be readily visible in *Doctor Who* until much later.

Between 1984 and 1989, when classic-era *Doctor Who* came to an end with the story 'Survival', the Doctor spent very little time confronting or even using computers. They were visible as set dressing in a few stories, but little more than that, save perhaps for the inclusion of an early code-breaking machine in 'The Curse of Fenric', used more as a convenient plot device than as a computer *per se*. However, in the gap in broadcasts between 'Survival' and 'Rose', which launched the revived *Doctor Who* in 2005, technology changed drastically, and the programme would change right along with it.

In 1989, it was not uncommon for a computer to be present in the home, usually consigned to a home office or at least a desk in a corner of the living-room. The computer itself was probably using a GUI like the Macintosh's, although by this point it was increasingly some variant of the Windows operating system. Most users could turn the machine on, navigate the screen with the mouse and at least get to a word-processing or spreadsheet file and make something happen. A great many users were also surprisingly adept at Patience, commonly included with computer systems under the name Solitaire. That was it, though. While modems to connect computers over the telephone system had been around for decades prior to the 1990s, few people bothered to connect to anything if they even owned a modem. Computers were self-contained tools for a very specific set of jobs such as word-processing or desktop publishing, not the centre of everyday life.

What a difference a few years makes. By the end of 1995, it was an entirely different world for computers, and the uses to which they could be put. The catalyst for the change, or the triggering technology, was not so much the ability to network computers together, but having something to network to. The first efforts were enclave systems, such as America On-line, or AOL, a dial-up service in the US that grew its market tremendously by sending out floppy disks, and later CD-ROMs, with all the software necessary to get a computer to connect to it, and then giving those users something to do, such as compete in computer games, download small programs or images, or chat in various forums. The AOL set-up disks were so ubiquitous in the early 1990s that a savvy user might have never actually needed to buy floppy disks. But almost from the launch of AOL in 1991, the clock was ticking for its demise, due to a different development that had been lurking in the background for decades before.

The ARPANET had been around since the 1960s, growing out of a Cold War fear that military bases might be cut off from communications in the event of a nuclear war. The networking technology developed as a result of those early efforts to get computers to communicate with each other had grown enough by the 1980s that many universities and even some public facilities like libraries could connect to the ARPANET. But the technology was quite arcane, and required a substantial knowledge of commands and specific locations to be useful at all, so most of society did not use it, if they were even aware of it. That began to change in 1991, the same year AOL went live, as the first web browser was developed as a way of putting a GUI-like interface on the network. The first browser effort was little more than a test of the technology, but by 1993, the test was certainly successful when Mosaic, the first readily-available graphical web browser, came out and the 'dot com' bubble of the later 1990s began to inflate with alarming rapidity.

While Mosaic was designed to allow a user to surf what it called the world-wide web, very quickly the term most widely used became the internet. The number of websites mushroomed as more and more people got online with their computers. Modems were almost a requirement for a computer in the mid-1990s, and a new term, surfing the internet, entered the lexicon of the western world. Businesses flocked to the web, under the belief that a website was a requirement for success, even if that website offered little more than a logo and some flashy text. Of course, someone was going to figure out how to make money from all this. Two notable names were Amazon and eBay, both of which went online in 1995. Being able to shop via the internet, as well as being able to access information instantly through search engines such as Yahoo! and Google, changed the way people thought about technology.

By 2005, the year 'Rose' splashed across TV screens and *Doctor Who* began its meteoric rise to the status it holds today, society and computers were in a very different place than when the seventh Doctor and his companion Ace sauntered off into the sunset at the end of 'Survival', or even when Paul McGann as the eighth Doctor defeated the Master on American soil and sallied forth in his TARDIS in the 1996 TV movie. The world of 2005 was not quite the same as the world of today, but most of the pieces were in place, and the revived *Doctor Who* would show it. A global computer network was accepted as the norm, instantaneous informational access was expected, electronic commerce was commonplace, and receiving a telephone call in the middle of an open field was annoyingly frequent.

In this context, the revived *Doctor Who* features computers significantly less prominently, but far more ubiquitously, than the classic programme ever did. Most significant to this is the design of the TARDIS console room itself. In the early years of the 21st Century, there was a much deeper understanding among the general public of what computers could do, and they were so commonplace that it would have seemed rather bland to have the Doctor flying the TARDIS by mouse. Instead, there is a tacit acknowledgement of the need for digital technology, in the form of the surreptitiously-placed laptop and various monitors on the central console, but also an implication that computers alone would not be sufficient technology to enable travel through time and space. Even in the 1996 television movie, the console room had shifted from the classical bright white, digitally-run design of the 1980s to something much more akin to a Jules Verne-inspired design. It was darker and more brooding, a bit like a steampunk drawing-room might be, while the console layout had shifted from lots of keyboards and monitors back to more switches, knobs and arcane bits of vintage tech. Elements of this design theme were inherited by the revived programme in 2005, when Christopher Eccleston's ninth Doctor first showed his companion Rose inside the TARDIS. The console room of 2005 was vast compared with that of the classic programme, although the traditional wall roundels featured a little more prominently than in the 1996 version. The console itself was distinctly less computer-centric, with lots of cranks, knobs and switches, although there was a readily-visible laptop computer as part of the overall design.

The TARDIS interior changed little until David Tennant's tenth Doctor regenerated into Matt Smith's eleventh in 2010. The violent energy of that regeneration blasted the interior, and so a whole new design came about, fiercely retro in appearance. The console featured a small keyboard tucked under one section, and a decidedly retro-looking monitor, but also included very retro-tech bits such as dials, switches, foot pedals and something that looked rather like a brake-fluid reservoir from a car.

The most recent TARDIS console redesign for the fiftieth anniversary series and onward harks back more to the look of classic *Doctor Who*, although the central column has taken on the flair of a carousel, as parts of the ceiling rotate when the ship is in flight. The console features two flat-panel-style monitors but otherwise continues the trend of moving away from traditional keyboard-style computer interfaces to more 'mad scientist' controls, drawing back to the earliest ideas of the programme where time travel was a dangerous business and only the properly intelligent could manage the ship's operation, whereas anyone can use a computer.

Aside from the TARDIS, computer technology in the revived programme is ubiquitous, but seldom a significant plot issue. It is rare for the Doctor to interact directly with a computer, continuing the preference he expressed long ago in 'The Ice Warriors'. When he does use a computer, though, it is with blazing efficiency. Others, however, often use computers as a means to an end. From the very start of the revived series, the internet has played a role, as Rose seeks out a person who claims to have used it to find out the truth about the Doctor. A little later, in 'World War III', the Doctor uses his knowledge of the UNIT organisation's operations to direct Rose's boyfriend Mickey to blaze through layers of security with the password 'buffalo' and order a missile strike against the Slitheen invaders. In the same episode, the Doctor gives Mickey a computer virus that will eradicate his records from the internet, for safety. Later, in a rare case where the Doctor directly manipulates a computer system, during Matt Smith's debut story 'The Eleventh Hour', he manages to write a computer virus on a smartphone and get it pushed out through the internet to every digital and computer-driven counter in the world. Thus the role of the networked computer comes increasingly to the fore in the revived programme.

While the classic programme used a global network threat several times, and suggested that such a connection could be dangerous, by 2005 it was a *fait accompli*. The question the public was asking was, what exactly was out there on the internet?

COMPUTERS

Who were the hackers? Could a savvy user put the pieces together from disparate sources and find out more than they were supposed to, as happened in 'Rose'? With new technologies such as Google's Street View, introduced in 2007, some serious privacy concerns came up, although the habit of Googling oneself to see what is public record went back much further than that.[30] The concept of a computer virus was also pretty well understood and accepted by society in 2005, and several high-profile virus problems had left their mark by then, both in the computer systems of the world and in the media. So it was that by that time even the casual computer-user understood that networks were a mixed blessing, with both potential and threat, replete with bountiful information and nefarious hackers.

The universality of technology provides a key plot point for the Matt Smith story 'The Bells of Saint John'. In this episode, the Great Intelligence, a malign formless entity introduced in the second Doctor's era, is at work again, this time recording people as data; hacking human beings, as it were. Two themes are poignantly underscored in the episode. The first is that any human being can be a target, and that effectively there is no defence against the hack. Certainly this plays into the societal fear of identity theft, and the fear that a hacked computer can become a tool in larger hacks, as the frequent media reports about 'bot nets' indicate. The second theme this episode highlights is how widespread technology is. In the course of the story, the Great Intelligence tries to track the Doctor through London, and because of the incredibly prevalent use of mobile phones and other digital devices as video, photographic and audio recorders throughout the city, it quickly succeeds. But this, too, highlights the fear of having so much technology in the world around us. Is Google listening in? Is your mobile phone

---

[30] 'Google's street-level maps raising concerns.'
USA Today, 1 June 2007, accessed 31 December 2013. http://usatoday30.usatoday.com/tech/news/internetprivacy/2007-06-01-google-maps-privacy_N.htm

provider tracking you? How much data gets recorded when you ask your mobile phone for restaurant suggestions? And what could a nefarious force do with all that information? The Doctor, in the revived programme, acts as just such an ultra-hacker, only he works for good instead of ill. But manifest in his actions is the social concern: just how vulnerable to a hacker's influence are the computer systems and networks that so many depend on? There was, and continues to be, a general perception that a savvy computer hacker can, in a matter of seconds, do something dreadful. Given the ongoing spate of credit card number breaches, identity thefts, 'ransomware' apps, high-profile government data losses and even innocuous Facebook hacks, a certain degree of paranoia is perhaps justified. Fortunately, most attacks are not simple affairs, but are brute force efforts that either take time or rely on terribly weak passwords, unlike the five-second hack the Doctor appears capable of. At least *Doctor Who* seems to have been able to promote good password development after the 'buffalo' incident, if the more complex password 'rycbar123' that the Doctor's new companion Clara uses in 'The Bells of Saint John' is any indication.

The revival of *Doctor Who* brings back to viewers the social fears about computers, only now, instead of the computers themselves being the source of malice, the dominant theme is that someone frighteningly skilled in their operation could use them for malicious purposes. The computers of the 1960s were vast, forbidding, misunderstood oracles that were going to take over everyone's lives, and possibly eradicate mankind in the process. By the 1980s, computers were much more commonplace objects, and took an appropriate place in the programme, although there was still the inherent risk of computer-driven destruction, albeit with a human in control. By 2005, computers were ubiquitous, from desktops and laptops to internet-connected refrigerators. People had made their peace with the premise of the computer, and a majority of the population used one on a regular basis. But there was a fear that, for all their advantages, they could still be put to malicious use, and some powerful, hidden figure could wreak havoc with a few simple keystrokes. So far, society is still relatively safe. Many computer 'hacks' are the result of human error rather than really clever code, and while there certainly is a growing underground network of cybercriminals, as yet no-one has been able to crank out a virus on the spur of the moment that takes the whole world hostage. *Doctor Who* has been a safe and comfortable way for society to cope with the rise of the computer over the past 52 years, and this is one of the most directly visible ways it serves as a time machine for technological and social history.

DAVID JOHNSON

Life, Death and Technology

Immortality, or aspects of it, plays a notable and recurrent role in *Doctor Who*. Arguably the principal message from *Doctor Who* about true immortality is that it is a bad thing. The first Doctor, played by Richard Hurndall in the twentieth anniversary story 'The Five Doctors', is quite direct when he asserts, 'Rassilon knew immortality was a curse, not a blessing.' However, the number of true immortals – beings completely incapable of death – in *Doctor Who* is quite small, examples including the Celestial Toymaker and the Black and White Guardians in the classic programme, and Ashildr in the revived one. Indeed, the case of Ashildr serves as a strong affirmation of the costs of immortality, as her diaries and her presence at the literal end of the universe show. Instead of exploring these examples, a more instructive way to look at the idea of immortality is to focus on cases where beings have sought or managed to achieve an extremely extended lifespan. In this regard, *Doctor Who* most assuredly offers a great deal to consider, both in terms of the methods used to achieve the extended lifespan, and of the potential benefits and costs of such a lifespan.

In general terms, *Doctor Who* explores two methods of achieving a near-immortal life, both of which rely on a certain amount of technology, especially in the field of medicine. The first is through mechanical means, such as by replacing body parts with fresh ones or more frequently with cybernetic ones. The Cybermen are the classic example of this method of immortality. The second method is direct manipulation of the life-form itself to make it live longer, either through genetic alteration or some other change to the inherent biology. Typically, though not exclusively, this second method relies on a degree of medical technology to create the desired effect, although seldom is that effect properly achieved. The Doctor himself serves as the best example of this kind of biological immortality, albeit one with well-established limits. The 1966 serial 'The Tenth Planet' provides a nice overview of both methods, as it introduces both the Cybermen and the concept of the Doctor being able to regenerate – although it was not formally referred to as such until the 1974 serial 'Planet of the Spiders.'

In 'The Tenth Planet', a lost world that is Earth's mirror image reappears. This world, Mondas, starts to drain energy from the Earth, while its inhabitants, the nearly-immortal Cybermen, arrive and propose take humans back with them for conversion into new members of their race. The backstory given for the Cybermen is that, after Mondas drifted away from the solar system and into deep space, its scientists came up with replacement body parts for its inhabitants, weeding out emotion from the brain in the process. In one of the last really stirring moments for William Hartnell's portrayal of the Doctor, he challenges the Cybermen about this, asking, 'Emotions! Love, pride, hate, fear! Have you no emotions, sir?', to which a Cyberman replies, 'Come to Mondas and you will have no need of emotions. You will become like us.' The desire of the Cybermen to seek out humans to 'convert' or 'upgrade' would play out through both the classic and the revived *Doctor Who* programmes. The obvious implication of this exchange, and in fact of many appearances afterwards, is that this method of immortality using cybernetic parts has also cost the Cybermen their humanity. At the core of the idea of conversion is the question whether or not the benefits of medical technology would also come with a very high price.

The state of medical technology in 1966, and the underlying popular perceptions of it, put 'The Tenth Planet' into a better context. The medical advances of the 20th Century were indeed substantial, and the majority of them took place in the wake of the Second World War. While Louis Pasteur's germ theory dates back to the Victorian era, it was only in 1941 that organic penicillin was produced in sufficient quantities to be useful for clinical medicine, and only in 1957 that a more efficient inorganic synthesis of the drug was perfected.[31] Thus the field of antibiotics was still fairly fresh in 1966, and as yet the unfortunate aftereffects of drug resistance were not a concern. At least for adult viewers of *Doctor Who*, the notion of being able to take a pill to cure a host of different problems, from earaches to unpleasant 'social' diseases, was still remarkable. The development of the polio vaccine in the 1950s, and later vaccines for measles and other diseases, had further bolstered popular confidence in the continued success of medicine, and with it the promise of a better, longer life.

More significant, though, from a Cyberman perspective, were a number of surgical developments in the 1950s and 1960s. In 1954, Joseph Murray completed the first transplant of a human kidney, from one identical twin to another; and later research suggested non-related donors could lead to a successful transplant as well, so long as certain conditions were met.[32] Artificial hip replacement dates back to 1891, although a substantially refined technique was developed and popularised in the 1960s, making the surgery an option for many more people.[33] The use of large, external heart/lung machines dates back to the 1940s, but a large-scale effort to develop a workable artificial heart was under way by 1964, with a stated goal of having a workable implant by the end of the decade.[34] That goal

---

[31] John S Mailer and Barbara Mason. 'Penicillin: Medicine's Wartime Wonder Drug and Its Production at Peoria, Illinois.'
Northern Illinois University, accessed 5 January 2014. http://www.lib.niu.edu/2001/iht810139.html

[32] 'Milestones in Organ Transplantation.'
National Kidney Foundation, 2015, accessed 14 April 2015. https://www.kidney.org/transplantation/transaction/Milestones-Organ-Transplantation

[33] Ananya Mandel, MD. 'Hip Replacement History' *News Medical*, 16 October 2014, accessed 6 January 2015. http://www.news-medical.net/health/Hip-Replacement-History.aspx

[34] Jauhar Sandeep, MD, PhD. 'The Artificial Heart.' *New England Journal of Medicine* (2004): 542-544.

proved impossible to achieve at the time, but the promise of what technology could do for the human lifespan and the quality of that life seemed virtually boundless in the 1960s.

With the technological changes to medicine, a new term entered the English language: bionics. A critical distinction is necessary here, as the word cybernetics, as used by Dr Kit Pedler, has a very different meaning from the word bionics, even though the two are often seen as interchangeable. Cybernetics is a system of control and communication in which logic drives the actions necessary to create a desired outcome. As Dr Pedler and Gerry Davis envisioned the Cybermen in 1966, should logic dictate the need to kill an individual, that was the course of action they would take, and emotions would not be a factor in the action.[35] Bionics, applying mechanical methods to biological systems, can be incorporated into a cybernetic system, but can also exist independent of the overall structure that cybernetics implies. By the middle of the 1960s, research into bionic parts for humans was demonstrably under way, with the goal of creating more life-like prosthetic limbs.[36] But a tacit question in all of this was, what did it mean to be human? In part, this contributed to the creation of the Cybermen as a *Doctor Who* monster, as Dr Pedler was concerned about the dehumanisation of medicine in the 1960s.[37] This is not to say that there was a large Luddite population rallying against medical development. Nor did people with prosthetic limbs feel less human. Instead, there was a background awareness about possible costs in human terms if such technological developments were carried past a certain extreme, especially if those developments fell under a unified control system. The

---

[35] David Banks, 13.
[36] Peter Asaro. 'Heinz Von Foerster and the Bio-Computing Movements of the 1960s' in *An Unfinished Revolution: Heinz Von Foerster and the Biological Computer Laboratory, BCL, 1958-1976*, ed. Albert Müller, Karl H Müller. (Edition Echoraum, 2007), 257-259. PDF at http://www.stim.illinois.edu/unfinishedrev/11_asaro.pdf ----- totl pp(255-275)
[37] David Banks, 8.

threat the Cybermen posed in many of their appearances in *Doctor Who* was that they needed humans still at their core, and so threatened to make humans like them, whether humans wanted it or not. The Cybermen of 'The Tenth Planet' and later stories directly addressed the question of the role and price paid for mechanical immortality.

As for the Doctor's first regeneration, this is foreshadowed when he speculates at one point, 'This old body of mine is wearing a bit thin.' He even becomes quite ill during the course of the serial; a necessary last-minute plot modification to accommodate William Hartnell's own illness during the week of recording of episode three. At the end of episode four, as the Doctor hurries back to the TARDIS ahead of his companions, he is quite weak. He then collapses to the control room floor, where his body is bathed in a bright glow before a younger face appears: that of Patrick Troughton as the second Doctor. From a production point of view, the change was necessary as William Hartnell had been in increasingly frail health, due in part to the rigorous recording schedule of *Doctor Who*, and so it was a simple, pragmatic way to keep the programme on the air. The notion of a steady stream of companions in the TARDIS had been readily accepted by viewers, so it seemed plausible that invoking some sort of alien physiognomy for the Doctor to allow him to rejuvenate himself would also work with the audience. Pragmatics of the moment aside, this one event in *Doctor Who*'s history more than any other was responsible for the programme's survival for more than fifty years, granting it a kind of actor-independent immortality that few television dramas have. For all the significance of the transition, relatively little is made of it in the follow-up story, 'The Power of the Daleks'. There is some discussion about it between companions Ben and Polly, particularly in the first episode, and the new Doctor devotes a few moments to assessing his new face. But then he is simply off and running, managing to defeat a group of Daleks attempting to take over a human colony.

Inherent in the first regeneration, though, was a new question: is a purely biological rejuvenation or regeneration possible? Bluntly, in the 1960s, or even in 2016, the answer is no. But there are curious examples in the natural world of very-long-lived creatures, such as the sea turtle, and even of creatures that seem to be able to regenerate themselves when needed, such as the so-called immortal jellyfish.[38] Genetic research was still largely in its infancy when the Cybermen first appeared in *Doctor Who*, although the possibility of genetic manipulation was acknowledged. But as new swarms of Cybermen stampede across the screen in the revived programme, geneticists are tantalisingly close to identifying the genes that control ageing, and have even begun to explore means of turning back the biological clock. As with bionics, though, the question of possible cost comes up. Thus, in 'The Tenth Planet', both biological and technological means of immortality, defined at least as greatly extended life, are introduced in *Doctor Who*.

Many variations on the idea of technological immortality are explored in later Cyberman stories. Narratively, the destruction of Mondas at the end of 'The Tenth Planet' is a significant setback for the Cybermen, but not the end of them, as only four serials later they reappear in 'The Moonbase.' These Cybermen are from an alternate Cyberman planet, Telos. 'The Tomb of the Cybermen' marked the next appearance of the race, and a new twist on their potential threat to humanity. In this serial, an archaeological expedition has set out to find the tombs of the Cybermen, not seen for over five hundred years. The Doctor and his companions stumble into the mission just as the tombs are uncovered. Klieg, a master logician, wants to use Cybermen's power to assert control over the Earth, but of course, the Cybermen have other plans. The Cybermen have set certain traps, knowing someone would come looking for their tombs. These traps are essentially physical applications of computer hardware designs, such as the use of a logical OR gate

---

[38] The species in question is the Turritopsis dohrnii, and can revert from its adult state back to a sexually immature state, effectively regenerating in a cycle that could, potentially, go on indefinitely.

to control the doors and the main hatch, as well as running the weapons-room console. These tests were designed to ensure that only properly intelligent humans would be able to gain access to the Cybermen, so they would make more suitable conversions. Such tests also serve as a subtle exploration of the possibility that humans might eventually outsmart themselves, whether in medicine or in some other technical or scientific field, and find themselves trapped by their own actions. In the case of 'The Tomb of the Cybermen', the trap involves humans being used for conversion into more Cybermen.

Only one human is actually converted in the serial, and then only partly. A woman named Kaftan is in league with Klieg, and is the main funding source for the expedition. She has with her a very tall, burly servant, Toberman, and it is he who is inadvertently trapped in the Cyber-tombs and partially converted. Only Toberman's arms are physically changed, although apparently the Cybermen also affect his mind, as he follows their orders for most of the rest of the serial. In the end, though, because he is not completely converted, he is also the one who saves the day, fighting off the Cyber-Controller and sacrificing his life to seal the doors of the Cyber-tombs again. The underlying message in the portrayal of Toberman is that even with some degree of cybernetic implants, humanity can still win out over the machine element, given enough effort. There is even the implicit theme in Toberman's self-sacrifice that death as a human can be preferable to cyber-immortality.

The conversion motif is played out repeatedly in other Cyberman stories, often with the same general plot of some human wishing to gain control over humanity by exploiting Cyberman force or technology. In 'The Invasion', Tobias Vaughn has connected with the Cybermen through some means, and seeks to control the world while offering suitable specimens for his allies to convert. He himself has been partly converted, but his brain remains completely human at his insistence. As with 'The Tomb of the Cybermen', Vaughn ultimately rebels against the Cybermen to save humanity, at the cost of his own life. Similar themes can be found in both

'Revenge of the Cybermen' with Tom Baker's Doctor, and 'Attack of the Cybermen' with Colin Baker's. Repeatedly in the classic programme, the struggle is between mechanical and unfeeling immortality and the value of humanity, even if choosing humanity also means choosing death.

In the revived programme, a somewhat different Cyberman origin story plays out in a parallel universe in the two-part story 'Rise of the Cybermen' / 'The Age of Steel', although again this involves the conversion of human beings into partly mechanical creatures. Very familiar territory comes back around, as John Lumic, a terminally-ill man, has devoted his life to creating an 'upgrade' for the human race. At the time, executive producer Russell T Davies felt that the 1960s fear about organ replacement was not as relevant to a 21st Century audience, and so wanted to make the Cyberman threat more about the fact that the immortality an 'upgrade' could offer was 'uniform and emotionless.'[39] Thus, in the two-part story, Lumic is unwillingly converted into a Cyber-Controller and ultimately perishes in the flames of the Cyberman factory after the Doctor, with a fair amount of help from companions Rose and Mickey, defeats the Cybermen. Notably, the method the Doctor uses to do this is to unblock the emotional inhibitor the Cybermen have in them, with the result that the human-converted Cybermen cannot cope with their conversion and go insane.

The idea of emotion being incompatible with this sort of mechanical upgrade is reinforced by several revived-programme stories, including 'Closing Time' and 'Death In Heaven.' 'Closing Time' offers little fresh in the way of the Cybermen themselves, but does serve to introduce Stormageddon, otherwise known as Alfie Owens, the son of the bumbling but honourable Craig Owens. The bond between father and son serves as the means of defeating the Cybermen here, in a slightly over-the-top affirmation of Davies' new take

---

[39] 'Rise of the Cybermen (TV story)'
TARDIS Data Core, accessed 8 January 2014.
tardis.wikia.com/wiki/Rise_of_the_Cybermen_(TV_story)

on the Cybermen. A more dynamic and layered exploration of mechanical immortality plays out in the Series Eight closer, 'Death in Heaven.'

Throughout Series Eight, executive producer Steven Moffat had his writers develop and explore the relationship between companion Clara Oswald, played by Jenna Coleman, and Danny Pink, played by Samuel Anderson. In 'Death in Heaven', this tumultuous relationship seems to be reaching a climatic point, as Clara prepares to confess all to Danny about her adventures with the Doctor, but then Danny is senselessly killed. Death in *Doctor Who* is not necessarily the end, though, as has been repeatedly affirmed during the series, when various people killed during the stories have found themselves in Heaven. Heaven, of course, is not really an afterlife, but a bit of stolen Time Lord technology that serves as a sort of psychic cloud for the minds of the deceased, while their dead bodies are upgraded into Cybermen. It is in this capacity that Danny Pink comes back to the fore.

Once his body is upgraded, Danny bravely chooses not to activate the emotional inhibitor that will complete the conversion process, despite this leaving him in essentially the same tormented state that destroyed the Cybermen in 'Rise of the Cybermen' / 'The Age of Steel'; he repeatedly says, 'I don't want to feel like this.' The story serves as a sharp affirmation that the potential for cybernetic immortality is incompatible with basic human emotional needs, a point doubly reinforced by the spectacular self-destruction of the new Cyberman army once put under Danny Pink's control, and by the final 'appearance' of Brigadier Lethbridge-Stewart as another Cyberman not fully under Cyber Control. The outcome of the story is a bit ironic, though, inasmuch as the human minds that are so discontent as Cybermen seem perfectly at ease within the virtual world created by the Time Lord technology in Heaven.

Doctor Who is treading here on familiar ground within the world of science fiction. The groundbreaking film and later television series *Max Headroom* was based on the notion that a human mind could be digitally translated into a computer and still continue to function as an independently-thinking entity. Later, the series *Red Dwarf* explored a slightly different take on this concept with the use of a hologram character, the mind of which was run on the ship's computer thanks to a 'personality disc'. In both shows, there are subtle questions about who the 'real' character is. Is Max Headroom, the digital entity, the same as Edison Carter, the man from whom he was derived? More poignantly, in *Red Dwarf*, more than one story considers whether or not the hologrammatic version of Arnold Rimmer is actually the same as the real, if deceased, Arnold Rimmer. In this context, in *Doctor Who* the question of cybernetic immortality does not focus on the possibility of such a thing existing, or even on the question of who the real character is, but instead offers a way of considering whether or not such a state would be desirable.

Doctor Who has further explored this theme of virtual immortality using one of the most remarkable and highly popular figures of the revived programme – River Song. River is the creation of Steven Moffat, who wrote her first appearance before he became executive producer. In a two two-part serial, 'Silence in the Library' / 'Forest of the Dead', viewers got a taste of what was to come for the Moffat era of *Doctor Who*, as River and the Doctor encounter each other from opposite ends of their own personal timestreams, wherein their first meeting from both the Doctor's point of view and the viewers' is the last from River's perspective. In subsequent episodes, River and the Doctor routinely compare notes to see where they are in their relative timelines, so as to avoid 'spoilers' and not give away too much about the future; but in 'Forest of the Dead', this problem is particularly acute for River, as the episode ends with her death. Or rather, as with Danny Pink, the episode ends with her *physical* death. A plot device within the story provides an 'out' for River through the use of virtual immortality.

The main action of the story is set in the greatest library in the universe, so vast that it is simply known as 'the Library'. It is apparently deserted when the tenth Doctor arrives with his companion Donna Noble, but he detects millions of non-human life-forms. These life-forms turn out to be Vashta Nerada, shadow beings that eat flesh. In order to spare the patrons of the Library from this fate, a computer system built to house the mind of a dying little girl has saved them all in a vast virtual world. As part of the climactic struggle to fend off the Vashta Nerada and bring the patrons back into the real physical world, River forces the Doctor to let her take his place for a biological computer uplink, which proves to be fatal. However, a device known as a neural relay has been shown through the story to keep an imprint of its user's mind even after death, and a neural relay in the sonic screwdriver previously given by the Doctor to River allows him to upload her into the Library computer system, giving her an effective virtual immortality.

So far, there is little new in this application of virtual immortality relative to earlier efforts such as *Max Headroom*. However, the Series Seven finale 'The Name of the Doctor' puts a twist on things, and raises new questions about the role of a virtual reality existence. In this episode, Clara is summoned to a psychic 'conference call' with the Doctor's Silurian ally Madame Vastra and her crew in Victorian London, as well as River Song. This, at first, is not terribly extraordinary, as River has popped up at odd intervals throughout the past couple of series. But it turns out that this is the 'dead' River, linked into the call through her virtual existence in the Library. At the story's climax, the Doctor is preparing to save Clara from being scattered forever across his own timestream, after she jumps into it to thwart the Great Intelligence. First, though, he has a poignant exchange with River, commenting on her continued existence. He says she is 'an echo' that 'should've faded by now'. In that assessment, there is a whole new layer of consideration to the immortality problem. Is a virtual immortality desirable, if such a thing were even possible? Would being a cognisant computer sprite be satisfying as an existence? And, more to the point, as the Doctor asks, what would be the value of such an existence? For some, perhaps the benefit of preserving their experience as a reference could be useful. But there are limits there, too. If the mind of Albert

Einstein had been preserved in some sort of *Futurama*-esque head in a jar, would it be able to cope with the latest developments in quantum mechanics, the inflationary theory of the universe and the problems of dark matter and dark energy? Would the limits of Einstein's experiences while he was in a physical body make such a conversation too difficult? Or, perhaps worse, would a virtual immortality create the same sort of stasis the Sisterhood of Karn suffers?

The Sisterhood of Karn offer an exploration of the other aspect of immortality that percolates through *Doctor Who*; a purely biological immortality along the lines of the Doctor's ability to regenerate. The classic-era serial 'The Brain of Morbius' offers a Time Lord take on the Frankenstein story. The criminal Time Lord Morbius's brain has been preserved while surgeon Solon attempts to fashion a new body for it from spare parts salvaged from different spacecraft crashes on the planet Karn. Effectively, Morbius is attempting to achieve through Solon a mechanical regeneration, as his body has been destroyed, so he can no longer regenerate as other Time Lords can. As the story unfolds, Solon wants to complete the body by using the Doctor's head to house Morbius's brain, but of course the Doctor is not too keen on the idea, and so fights back. With the help of the Sisterhood of Karn, a group of women given perpetual life by an Elixir of Life that comes from stones heated by a flame from a geothermal vent, the Doctor is able to defeat Morbius in a sort of mental duel, and then Morbius's cobbled-together body is driven over a cliff by the Sisterhood.

In 'The Brain of Morbius', the Frankenstein's Monster-like body of Morbius represents a simplistic gross misapplication of surgical technology not too far removed from the Cybermen, and serves as a reminder that perhaps life at all costs is not the best idea. But the Sisterhood of Karn offer something else. They achieve a biological immortality through the consumption of the Elixir of Life, but at a serious cost – at least from the Doctor's point of view. The Elixir is well known to the Time Lords, and the Sisterhood have previously been quite willing to share it with them for the use of those suffering 'post-regenerative trauma', but the flame that burns to create it has been faltering lately, so the supply is very low. The Doctor asserts that the Elixir is nothing terribly special, and that with a good spectrographic analysis it could be made 'by the gallon', but that it doesn't need to be. There is a stasis or stagnation that comes with this type of immortality, where nothing ever changes. There is a significant social question in the Doctor's assertion. Would a person want eternal life in a world that never changed? Put another way, would immortality sound quite so enjoyable if it meant an immortality of the same nine-to-five job and tending the garden on weekends? While Time Lords are long-lived, they are not entirely immortal, and cannot even continue to regenerate indefinitely – they are normally limited to 13 incarnations. They also change their personality, and sometimes even their gender, with each regeneration, making the Doctor's disdain for the Sisterhood of Karn more plausible from a narrative perspective.

Despite feeling no fondness for the chemically-supported biological immortality the Sisterhood have, the Doctor does clear the block in their geothermal vent, using a firecracker, and leaves two more firecrackers with them for use in the event it clogs up again. This proves fortunate for one of his later incarnations. In the revived programme mini-episode 'The Night of the Doctor', the eighth Doctor as portrayed by Paul McGann crashes back on Karn. The Doctor refers to his rescuers as the 'keepers of the flame of utter boredom', in an echo of his previously established disdain for their form of immortality, but finds that he needs them, as he is in fact dead, and requires their help to force a regeneration within the next four minutes. The lead Sister asserts that Time Lord technology has reached a pinnacle on Karn, offering the Doctor a choice of attributes in his new incarnation. For the purposes of the narrative developed for the programme's fiftieth anniversary, the Doctor needs to be a 'warrior' to battle against the Daleks during the Time War, and so he chooses a potion from the Sisterhood that regenerates him into the War Doctor as played by John Hurt. Both narratively, and perhaps even ethically, this is a suitable application of Time Lord technology; but the classic series offered two serials where Time Lord technology for immortality was misapplied, and showed the consequences of that.

The serials 'Underworld' with the fourth Doctor and 'Mawdryn Undead' with the fifth present a darker view of what misapplied biological immortality can do, although in both cases specific Time Lord technology is used to create the biological effect. In 'Underworld', the Doctor lands on the decrepit spacecraft R1C, which is carrying a search crew from the Minyan civilisation, seeking the genetic databanks of their people that were lost after their planet was destroyed. The Minyans are familiar with the Doctor's people from the earliest days of their history, when the Time Lords gave them the means to regenerate indefinitely, a sort of mechanical variant on the Sisterhood of Karn's Elixir of Life. But the Minyans' minds do not always cope well with this harsh sort of immortality, as seen when one of the crew waits almost too long to regenerate herself and nearly dies, because she is so tired of the endless quest they are on. In the story, the Doctor says that the Time Lord policy of non-intervention came into being because their efforts with the Minyans went so poorly. Ironically, this policy is sometimes alluded to by the Doctor as one of the reasons he left Gallifrey, as their society was falling into a stasis much like that of the Sisterhood on Karn. Indirectly, the policy of non-intervention is a Time Lord admission that even the best-laid plans can go terribly wrong; a message that might have resonated well with viewers in the mid-1970s, when the first discussions of cloning and concerns about increasing problems in medical care were popping up in the news occasionally.

'Mawdryn Undead' drew on these concerns by presenting a group of aliens who stole Time Lord technology to achieve immortality. The attempt went horribly wrong, leaving Mawdryn and his companions undergoing perpetual regeneration, but in great pain and unable to effect any change in their condition. Perhaps a fair analogy to this is the situation a cancer patient finds himself or herself in when the therapies used to fight the cancer do prolong life, but at the cost of a great decrease in quality of life. In the story, the Doctor is asked to give up all his remaining regenerations to bring about the deaths of the aliens, a fate they desire. Fortunately for him, a bit of technobabble referred to as the Blinovich limitation effect comes into play at just the right moment. Two version of Brigadier Lethbridge-Stewart meet up just as a machine is about to drain off the Doctor's regenerations, and the temporal paradox creates a tremendous burst of energy, allowing the aliens to die while still preserving the Doctor's regenerations. Despite the happy ending, the message is clear: there could be remarkably unforeseen complications with medical technology, even if its original purpose or intent was noble.

In the early 1980s, some of the limitations and problems of medicine were increasingly coming to the fore. Most prominently, a new disease was being widely discussed at the time; a disease first named only four months before the February 1983 broadcast of 'Mawdryn Undead'. We know of it most commonly by its acronym, AIDS, which stands for Acquired Immunodeficiency Syndrome, and the first traceable use of that term came on 24 September 1982.[40] Misinformation about ADIS during the 1980s was rampant, and public perceptions of the disease based on that misinformation are key to considering the social history of medicine in the 1980s. The most common misperceptions were that the disease could be transmitted through casual contact, that it was a 'gay' disease, and that it was invariably fatal. From a 21st Century perspective, it is demonstrably the case that none of these things is true. But in the context of some of the borderline hysteria of the early 1980s, AIDS was seen as a new sort of plague, and one that medical science could do little about. The public saw AIDS as a poignant indication of just how limited medicine was, and how far off any prospect of immortality might be.

The revived programme has added some new twists to the immortality issue. The character Cassandra, featured in both

---

[40] 'A Timeline of AIDS.' *AIDS.gov*, accessed 8 January 2014. http://aids.gov/hiv-aids-basics/hiv-aids-101/aids-timeline/

'The End of the World' and 'New Earth', provides a fresh approach to the consideration of what it means to be human. Cassandra is presented as little more than a sheet of skin with a face on it, boasting in 'The End of the World' that she has recently had her chin completely removed. In light of some of the highly-publicised and occasionally botched plastic surgeries of the late 20th and early 21st Centuries, the parallel here is obvious. The changing faces of diverse celebrities and the host of online images of people with unnatural bulges after bungled enhancement surgeries are still readily visible. In this context, Cassandra allowed for a consideration and even a satirisation of such social trends. Her boasting of being the last 'pure' human and the upbraiding Rose gives her in 'The End of the World' serve primarily as a reaffirmation of the same theme explored in the Cyberman stories, that immortality at the cost of humanity is not worth it. In the Doctor's second encounter with Cassandra, in a giant hospital on New Earth, *Doctor Who* offers a variant on the common theme of immortality: there is a natural time for everything to die. Cassandra, who has taken over Rose's body in an effort to stay alive, is reluctant to accept this truth, but when she finally switches over to a 'volunteer' body, and that body begins to fail, she does accept the reality of death. With the end of Cassandra comes an affirmation that technology should not be used to prolong life indefinitely, even if it were to become possible to do so.

The story 'The Lazarus Experiment' serves as a second affirmation of the idea of there being a natural time for death. In this, Professor Richard Lazarus claims he has invented a machine that will 'change what it means to be human'. The machine Lazarus has constructed appears to rejuvenate him, allowing the elderly professor to emerge as a young man again, although Doctor is certain he has not accounted for every possible variable. Of course, the Doctor is right, and latent segments of Lazarus's DNA transform him into a sort of scorpion-like energy vampire, draining life from others in order to stay alive. Near the climactic battle, the Doctor confronts Lazarus, asserting, 'Facing death is part of being human. You can't change that.' Lazarus responds, 'No, Doctor. Avoiding death, that's being human. It's our strongest impulse: to cling to life with every fibre of being.' Perhaps both ideas are correct for the human race. Most humans are reluctant to die, and many exert great effort to prevent death for as long as possible. Humans also recognise that eternal life, or unnaturally prolonged life, could come with a price that is too high, and that life at all costs might not be worthwhile in the end – as the recent spate of 'right to die' lawsuits and high-profile media stories about them have shown.

The consideration of immortality has changed substantially over the course of the fifty-odd years of *Doctor Who*, always in response to changes in the technology or science of the times. In the 1960s, medical technology appeared to be capable of great things, through organ transplants and the possibility of artificial parts much more lifelike than the clunky prosthetic limbs that had been around since at least the 19th Century. But what would a physical immortality be like? How many parts could be replaced before the essential aspects of the person who was being 'upgraded' became less human, or not human at all? Would an emotionless life be worthwhile? As the 1980s began, there were fresh concerns over whether or not medicine was trustworthy, and whether or not all the possible permutations of medical technology had been fully understood before it was applied to people. As such, *Doctor Who* explored what happens when technology is misapplied in the quest for immortality, echoing the social concerns of the day. And in the early 21st Century, there have been questions about the costs of immortality in a different sense, exploring the possibilities of conformity that could come with physical immortality with a new generation of Cybermen, but also considering the potential and the costs of an eternal virtual existence. Recurrently in the revived programme, the Doctor has asserted that there is a time and place for everything to end, that death has a place in the universe. It is perhaps ironic, then, that when the Doctor's own time appeared to be up in 'The Time of Doctor', when he was out of regenerations and had aged substantially on the planet

LIFE, DEATH AND TECHNOLOGY

Trenzalore, instead of dying at the hands of the Daleks, he was given by the Time Lords the energy for a new regeneration cycle, effectively cheating his own death, and posing a few narrative questions. This may not be as ironic as it seems, though, as research into anti-ageing therapies and medicines is not just ongoing, but currently making tremendous breakthroughs, such as finding ways to renew muscular strength, and ways to slow down or even reverse ageing at the cellular level in tissue samples. Humans are not yet able to prevent death, but medical technology continues to explore the prospect, and so *Doctor Who* provides a necessary and timely way to consider just what society should do, in the event such a possibility becomes reality.

DAVID JOHNSON

Scientists and their Gadgets

The modern world is practically synonymous with gadgets. A quick look around any home will reveal a mix of things that are supposed to make life easier, ranging from the ubiquitous television remote control to the programmable coffee machine and even the internet-savvy door lock. This is hardly a new trend, though. Scanning through a Victorian-era periodical, one can find a similar host of 19th Century gadgets such as safety night lights, magic lantern slide-shows and hand-cranked 'organettes' that 'a mere child' could operate to make music.[41] However, the later part of the 20th Century is filled with interesting new devices, coming out of both science labs and ramshackle garages, all supposedly with the power to make life better. Mirroring that late 20th Century world, *Doctor Who* is equally filled with a host of gadgety devices. Some of these, such as the Doctor's sonic screwdriver, are emblematic of the programme itself. Others, such as a timey-wimey detector that goes *ding*, appear only once or twice in the run of episodes. Whatever the device, and however often it appears, *Doctor Who* provides viewers with a means of evaluating their own position on the latest contraptions from the labs and workshops of the world. More importantly, the programme also allows viewers to evaluate whether or not the scientists or engineers making those devices always have the public's best interests in mind.

Most new inventions and discoveries are met with a degree of scepticism when they are first announced. The telegraph, the radio and the television set were all met with

---

[41] Advertisements section. *The Strand Magazine*, November 1892. i-xii.

some degree of mistrust or misunderstanding at the time they first came out. In 1844, when Samuel Morse sent the first long-distance telegraph using Morse Code, he tapped out 'What hath God wrought?' referencing Numbers 23:23 in the Bible.[42] The message can be seen as an affirmation of Christian faith, but it also reflects an understanding that this method of sending and receiving data had the potential to change the world in profound ways that even its inventor could not foresee. Yet, by the 1850s, telegraph lines crisscrossed the landscape on both sides of the Atlantic, and the first effort to run a cable across the Atlantic had taken place. The value and possibilities of virtually instantaneous electronic telecommunications were simply too enticing, so the public quickly embraced the telegraph, so much so that in cinema and television the sound of the dots and dashes of Morse code is still emblematic of the rapid transmission of information. However, the telegraph is not entirely a fair test of society's willingness to embrace a new device, inasmuch as it required a trained operator, and was not commonly deployed in homes.

The development of radio technology is much more instructive in showing the means by which a piece of gadgetry becomes an indispensable household item. The core technology for radio goes back to experiments in wireless transmission in the 1880s.[43] Certainly some forward-looking pioneers saw the potential for radio both as a long-distance communication system and even as a means of entertainment in its early days, but it was not until the 1920s that the

---

[42] 'Samuel F B Morse Sent the First Telegraphic Message May 24 1844.' *America's Library*, accessed 12 February 2014.
http://www.americaslibrary.gov/jb/reform/jb_reform_morsecod_1.html
[43] 'A Short History of Radio.' *FCC*, winter 2003, accessed 21 January 2014.
http://transition.fcc.gov/omd/history/radio/documents/short_history.pdf

general public really engaged with radio.[44] This was due partly to a hiatus in development during the First World War, but partly also to the way the equipment was marketed. Prior to the mid-1920s, a radio was not a ready-made product, but something an inventor or home tinkerer would assemble from a mix of parts, and use primarily as a means to talk to other radio owners about equipment, signal strength and technically arcane bits of relevant information. It was not a mainstream product by any means. However, as efforts at regular radio broadcasting for entertainment purposes took shape early in the 1920s, led by the Radio Corporation of America (RCA) in the United Stated and the British Broadcasting Company (BBC) in the UK, manufacturers realised there was a market for ready-made radios that could simply be plugged in and used. The explosive growth the radio market saw in the 1920s is indicative of how something can move from a gadget to an expected home appliance to a ubiquitous device that permeates through every level of society.[45] The development of transistor radios in the 1960s further demonstrated just how quickly a device that was once the purview of early electronics geeks could become something used almost everywhere, from the home to the car to the seafront resort.[46]

Television went through a similar growth curve, although a much quicker one, as the way to rapid adoption had already been paved by radio. The first experiments date to the 1920s,

---

[44] Thomas H White. 'Broadcasting After World War I (1918-1921).' *earlyradiohistory.us*, and Thomas H White. 'Big Business and Radio (1915-1922).' *earlyradiohistory.us*,
accessed 22 January 2014. http://earlyradiohistory.us/sec016.htm and http://earlyradiohistory.us/sec017.htm

[45] ibid and 'History of the BBC.' *BBC*, accessed 22 January 2014. http://www.bbc.co.uk/historyofthebbc/resources/factsheets/1920s.pdf

[46] Ryan Deal. 'Hottest Gadgets of the 1960s.' *Techvert*, 18 June 2010, accessed 13 January 2014. http://www.techvert.com/gadgets-of-the-1960s/

and experimental broadcasts were under way by the 1930s – although, as with radio before, much of the effort was interrupted by global conflict, in this case the Second World War. In the 1950s, the 'fad' of television really took off, as commercially-produced television sets and regular broadcasts moved it from experimental gadgetry to a mainstay of the living-room. By the time *Doctor Who* premiered in 1963, television had become a dominant social force. Few by that point would have considered a television set a gadget, and most saw it as a staple of the properly-equipped home. Tellingly, though, in 1963 very few people understood how a television set worked, beyond knowing it required electricity and probably needed a few minutes to warm up properly for the best possible picture. When the BBC made its switch in the late 1960s from the early 405-line broadcast format that saw *Doctor Who* through its first few series to the 625-line PAL format, most people would have understood only that they needed a new set to benefit fully, as the BBC had made television better.[47] As people tuned in to *Doctor Who* on their now appliance-like televisions throughout the 1960s, they saw the Doctor use a range of gadgets that suggested a better, easier future, although a future that was not without its perils.

Certainly one of the most iconic gadgets the Doctor uses is the sonic screwdriver, the evolution of which offers striking insights into society's perceptions of the latest contraption. Its first appearance in the chronology of the programme is in the now-lost Patrick Troughton serial 'Fury from the Deep', transmitted in 1968. Here it does exactly what its name would imply: it opens up a hatchway that is screwed shut. It is also used in this conventional way, to open control panels and remove screws, in the lengthy serial 'The War Games'. Although at one point in 'The Dominators' it is pressed into service as a cutting device, presumably through some sort of

---

[47] 'Early Colour Television.'
Early Television Museum, accessed 12 February 2014. http://www.earlytelevision.org/british_ntsc_color.html

sonic resonance, its usage in these late-1960s stories is fairly consistent with the original statement of its function, as an alien screwdriver.

With the arrival of the third Doctor in 1970, the sonic screwdriver began to change. In physical appearance it went from a simple penlight-like device to a larger instrument. The sonic screwdrivers for the third, fourth and fifth Doctors all featured a large head somewhat akin to a hollowed-out radar dish, while the handle went through several iterations that presumably introduced different kinds of controls for it. Perhaps as a result of the revisions to the device's physical form, more functions were also added to it. In addition to serving as an actual screwdriver to open access panels and the like, it was used to detect other electronic devices, to detonate landmines remotely, and even, at one point in 'Carnival of Monsters', to create a spark to ignite flammable gases. All these functions are at least possible extensions of the general concept of a sonic device, even if they are implausible. It is possible that a powerful enough signal at the right frequency could trip a mine, or even in some way indicate the presence of an electronic device, perhaps by creating or detecting a resonant frequency in one of the materials used to build that device. It is even remotely possible that a strong sonic pulse could create a wave powerful enough to compress flammable gas to the point of combustion, based on Boyle's Law.[48] Again, these operations of the sonic screwdriver were at least plausible within the original function of the device, although they did begin to strain credibility.

The development of the sonic screwdriver in the late 1960s and early 1970s approximately followed that of other home gadgets during the time period. New conveniences were being

---

[48] Boyle's Law describes the relationship between temperature and pressure for gases. Extrapolating from the law, is it at least theoretically possible to put a flammable gas under enough pressure that it might combust if mixed with oxygen. Boyle's Law is also the source of a terrible pun in the 1964 story 'The Dalek Invasion of Earth'.

developed and sold regularly, including the first electric shavers in 1967 and the first microwave ovens in the 1970s.[49] These devices represented a quantum leap over earlier methods, at least theoretically. The electric razor was supposed to offer a faster, smoother, safer shave, while the microwave oven offered a faster way to cook things or reheat leftovers. Both evolved a little bit from their original design, with the electric razor exploring variations in blade styles and the microwave oven gaining a timer function and more cooking modes, but for the most part they stayed true to their original form and function. In 1974, no-one realistically expected a microwave oven to function also as a telephone, or as a coffee percolator.

The problem of form and function was more pronounced in *Doctor Who*, though. A bit of a crisis with the sonic screwdriver developed in the programme during the later 1970s and early 1980s. The addition of a remarkably adept lock-picking capability to the things it could do didn't seem terribly worrisome, although it began to move beyond the earlier, more plausible functions of the device. Sonic locks requiring a specific tone to open had been around in *Doctor Who* since 'The Power of the Daleks' in 1966, but using sound to pick a mechanical lock was a substantially different application of the sonic screwdriver. This adding on of seemingly unrelated functions mirrored the evolution of gadgetry at that time, when, thanks to digital technology, combinations of functions were becoming the norm. The alarm clock was now also a radio, while the coffee pot could also serve as a clock. While far outside its previous functions, the fact that the sonic screwdriver is used as a delta-wave augmentor to help the Doctor's companion Nyssa sleep during the 1982 story 'Kinda' should thus come as no great surprise. It does, however, serve to highlight the crisis the device created for the programme. This unusual usage was written into the story in part because the Doctor needed to be

---

[49] Ryan Deal. 'Hottest Gadgets of the 1960s.' *Techvert*, 18 June 2010, accessed 13 January 2014. http://www.techvert.com/gadgets-of-the-1960s/

deprived of the sonic screwdriver, so that his imprisonment in the human explorers' base on the Kinda planet would be more significant. There is little drama in being imprisoned if the prisoner has a universal key. This issue was what drove producer John Nathan-Turner to have the device destroyed during the following serial, 'The Visitation.' The sonic screwdriver had become a sort of technological *deus ex machina*, where a writer could simply add a new function as the story demanded.

From 'The Visitation' through the end of the classic programme in 1989, the Doctor remained without a sonic screwdriver. The 1996 TV movie saw the return of the device in the hands of seventh Doctor Sylvester McCoy and eighth Doctor Paul McGann, though it was used little in the action and appeared to have much the same kind of functions as during the Pertwee era. With the revived programme, though, the sonic screwdriver became a remarkable and extremely versatile device. In design, it reverted to something closer to the original penlight form, but its function was greatly expanded. In addition to opening locks and doors and cutting or exploding various things, it now seems to act as a sort of universal remote control for a whole host of different technology, from computers to mobile phones to the TARDIS itself. It also serves as a highly versatile and adaptable scanning device. At one time or another, it has been able to hack into a mobile phone; bypass a security system; serve as a complex medical scanner capable of spotting changes in DNA; detect and monitor a host of signals, including telepathic signals; map the topography of the ocean floor; disable teleport devices; and turbo-charge a robot – among many other things. It also seems to be its own complex computational device, capable of running for over 400 years a subroutine that could have allowed it to resonate a door in the Tower of London out of existence, as seen in the fiftieth anniversary special 'The Day of the Doctor'. Given all the sonic screwdriver's features in the revived programme, it is possible to argue that it has become exactly the sort of *deus ex machina* device that John Nathan-Turner sought to destroy; an easy out for the Doctor in almost any situation.

There is a counterargument to this claim, though, and it has to do with how much technology and gadgetry have evolved in recent years. An internet meme that periodically makes it way around social media sites shows two pictures. The top one is labelled 1995, and shows various items such as a large and brick-like mobile phone, a bulky laptop computer, a film-based camera, a video camera, a rolodex card file, and so on. The bottom image is usually labelled to the current year and shows a single smartphone device. The meme is intended to be humorous, but it also makes a remarkable point. A handheld device of 2016 has more power, capability and function to it than a fully-fledged computer had in the late 1990s, and can serve as a perfectly suitable still or video camera, play myriad video and audio files, track thousands of personal contacts, access the sum total of the internet, and even make a phone call if the signal is good enough. There are even active efforts to allow a smartphone to function much like *Star Trek*'s medical tricorder, and plans are freely available through the internet to allow the smartphone camera to function as a moderate microscope or even a spectrograph. Granted, a mobile phone is as yet unable to hold back a Dalek or reprogram a Cyberman weapon, but there are at least a few people who seem to brandish theirs in the same manner as Matt Smith's Doctor wielded his sonic screwdriver, as if the sheer power of technology is enough to hold something at bay.

While the sonic screwdriver is arguably the most iconic and recognisable piece of gadgetry in *Doctor Who*, it is by no means the only one, and other, less universal devices offer insight into how social perceptions of scientists and their inventions have shifted substantially over time. Throughout the 1960s, the Doctor represented a sort of universal tinkerer, able quickly to assess any bit of technology and turn it to his own ends if needed. As previously noted, the first Doctor was able to reprogram one of the War Machines in that eponymous serial so that it attacked WOTAN. In 'The Web of Fear', the second Doctor is faced with two remarkable bits of technology, but converts both of them. The first is the control sphere of a robot Yeti, which he is able to alter so that it responds to voice controls from him instead of taking orders from the Great Intelligence. Later in the serial, as he is being led to a pyramidal machine that the Great Intelligence plans to use to extract his mind, he alters the brain-draining helmet in a matter of seconds, so that it will operate in reverse, draining the Great Intelligence into his mind instead (although this scheme is ultimately thwarted by the well-intentioned but mistaken intervention of his friends). In each case, the Doctor easily manages to change around some scientific gadget so that it serves his ends, as would be an expected outcome in the 1960s for someone with suitable scientific knowledge.

Given the state of technology in the 1960s, such actions were at least remotely plausible, if unlikely. For example, if an adventurous soul were to prise the back off a television set in 1965, there were readily visible parts inside that could conceivably be reordered into some other configuration. Granted, there would be a risk of severe electrical shock or worse, but someone with the Doctor's knowledge and the brain power could at least try to get better reception for the football match. The inner workings of 1960s gadgets were still highly visible, and to someone with a trained mind or eye, the distorted top of a capacitor or a blackened vacuum tube was a sure visual indicator of how to repair such a gadget. Little thought was given to changing a television into a microwave oven, however, or a death ray.

What if someone had been able to develop a death ray type of gadget? The potential for technology during the 1960s and 1970s seemed virtually boundless, and *Doctor Who* certainly explored exciting and dangerous possibilities. Examples included a weather-controlling gravity device called a gravitron in 'The Moonbase', and a teleportation device known as T-mat in 'The Seeds of Death'. In both cases, while there is tremendous benefit for mankind, there is also tremendous potential for destruction with the misapplication of the device. In the case of the gravitron, properly applied it can keep a hurricane at bay and guarantee suitable weather for farming. However, a few degrees difference in its alignment and the weather patterns on Earth shift catastrophically, leading to destruction, power shortages and other problems. While on one level the gravitron represents the solution to the adage 'Everyone talks about the weather, but no-one does anything about it', the trust presupposed by such a device is tremendous and potentially thought-provoking. The humans on Earth in 2070 – the year in which the story is set – must presumably turn a blind eye to the risk the technology would pose in the wrong hands, and have complete trust that the scientists and crew on the Moonbase will use it only as a benefit. A similar case is featured in 'The Seeds of Death', where the T-mat device can instantly transport anything from one location to another, using a lunar station as a relay point. The benefits of such technology would be incredible, to be certain. Food, medical supplies, even doctors and technicians, could be instantly available anyplace in the world a T-mat station was set up. A world-class heart surgeon in London could in a matter of seconds arrive in rural Colorado for an emergency surgery. Wheat crops from the steppes of Asia could instantly be sent to Europe, Africa or South America, saving both tremendous costs of transportation and also time. Of course, as with the gravitron, the potential to misuse such a device is also nearly boundless. Potentially lethal material could be sent just as quickly as beneficial material, as the Ice Warriors demonstrate in the serial, sending fungal spores all over the world to make Earth more like Mars. With both technologies, there is tremendous trust placed in the hands of those operating the devices, only to do good.

It would be tempting to see both of these devices as a commentary on the threat of nuclear holocaust that pervaded the 1960s. There are certainly grounds for that evaluation, as the Cold War reached an early pinnacle in 1961 with the construction of the first Berlin Wall, and in 1962 with the Cuban Missile Crisis. Later developments with the Vietnam conflict and the US's involvement in it did little to ease matters. However, it may not be fair to see these kinds of *Doctor Who* devices as analogues of nuclear weapons. Perhaps they should be viewed more as a commentary on other nuclear technology. The 1960s also saw a rapid rise in the use of nuclear power, with the first reactor in the UK coming on line in Cumbria in 1959.[50] At the time, nuclear power plants were considered to be a marked improvement over coal-fired electrical plants, and even now they are generally safer and cleaner than the latter. The problem, not yet a reality in the 1960s, is that if an accident does occur at a nuclear plant, it is likely to be far more serious and dangerous than one in a coal-fired plant. The potential doomsday scenarios of 'The Moonbase' and 'The Seeds of Death' are more akin to society reaching a peace with tremendously powerful scientific gadgetry that could be a great benefit, but could also be a great danger, and asking questions about trust. Are people willing to trust the scientists, or the government, with such powerful new devices, despite the risks? Do the scientists actually understand the risks?

A third Doctor serial adds to this with a new question. Instead of asking about trust, or if a new device is worth the risk, 'The Time Monster' poses the question, 'Have you really thought it through?' The device in question is referred to as TOMTIT, standing for Transmission of Matter through Interstitial Time. Effectively, this has much the same premise as the transmat device from 'The Seeds of Death'. However, there is a new element introduced here, in the form of Kronos, a sentient being in the time vortex. Much of the story is typical boilerplate *Doctor Who*, with lots of double-crosses and dramatic episode cliffhangers, and it is hard not to realise that things are going to go badly when, in the first episode, the inventor of the TOMTIT, Professor Thascales, is immediately recognised as the Master. That aside, there is a poignant question in the serial: what are the risks of misunderstood technology? Have the

---

[50] '1956: Queen switches on nuclear power.' *BBC News*, 2007, accessed 23 February 2014.
http://news.bbc.co.uk/onthisday/hi/dates/stories/october/17/news id_3147000/3147145.stm

designers really thought through all the possible consequences?

Historically, there is some precedent here. When the US's atomic-focused Manhattan Project was preparing to detonate the first atomic weapon in the world, there was a minor concern that the reaction would not be controllable, and would keep expanding until it vaporised the whole surface of the Earth. Obviously, the test went ahead despite the admittedly minimal risk. Marie Currie's use of radium is another atomic event wherein the discovering scientist did not fully understand the implications of the discovery. Had she fully grasped the impact of radiation on the human body, it is unlikely she would have kept a glowing radium sample on her bedside table as a night light. More recently, people have asked questions about how much understanding the scientists and controllers of other experiments have had. The Large Hadron Collider has been deemed a threat to the existence of the world both times it has started up, most recently for fear it would spawn a miniature black hole that would destroy the planet. With a modicum of reading, a person can understand that such black holes are indeed a possibility, but they would be on an atomic scale, and would dissipate almost as soon as they formed. However, the fear serves to underscore the societal need to ask questions about whether or not the scientists have thought through all the possibilities.

A number of other one-off devices in *Doctor Who* further build on the question of 'Have you thought it through?' In the Jon Pertwee serial 'Carnival of Monsters', the gadget in question assuredly falls into this category. It is known as a Miniscope, or more commonly just as a Scope, and it serves as a sort of portable electronic zoo, wherein various species are kept in self-contained environments, miniaturised for easy transportation using a compression field. There is one fairly obvious issue to consider with regard to the Scope, and that is the ethics of it being used to hold intelligent life-forms, most notably some humans captured while on board a 1920s cargo ship, the *SS Bernice*. Along this line, the Doctor notes the immorality of such devices, and that he was instrumental in getting them banned.

The central monster in 'Carnival of Monsters', a mindless and violent beast known as a Drashig, raises a larger question. In the story, some Drashigs are able to get out of their self-contained environment in the Scope, causing some internal damage to the device before later escaping the machine entirely. Once outside the compression field, they quickly assume their normal size and run amok on the planet before being blasted with an eradicator gun.

With the Drashig escape, the serial raises some prominent questions about the role of technological gadgetry in the early 1970s. It is fair to assert that in the context of *Doctor Who*, no-one in his right mind would attempt to transport Drashigs at full size. Such an action would be the *Doctor Who* equivalent of breeding velociraptors in *Jurassic Park*. Yet in 'Carnival of Monsters', Scope-owner Vorg thinks nothing of having the creatures tucked safely away in miniature, confident that the technology of the Scope will keep them from being a threat. At one point, Vorg even puts his hand directly into the Drashig enclosure to shoo them away from a sensitive area. It is outside of his thought process that the technology could somehow fail, and unleash a very real and very large threat. People from the 1970s onward have faced a similar consideration, inasmuch as society has become increasingly dependent on a host of technological gadgets and often gives little though to their possible failure. Granted, an electric razor is unlikely to go on a violent rampage when it fails, but the point about thinking through all the possibilities is still relevant, as a person might need to have an alternate means to shave before a major presentation, in the event that the electric razor does fail.

Many other serials in the classic programme explore similar themes of evaluating the gadgets or devices being used, and whether or not those devices have been properly thought through. Certainly the Jon Pertwee serial 'Inferno' is a direct consideration of this, evaluating whether or not the plan to drill deep into the Earth's crust is a good idea. Tom Baker's time in the TARDIS explores similar ideas in various ways, from the mechanical regeneration technology already noted in 'Underworld' to the use of a tachyon chamber in 'The Leisure

Hive'. Later 1980s episodes have less of this, but with the programme's return in 2005, new concerns about gadgets and the role of science came to the fore.

In the revived programme, there is certainly no shortage of gadgets. As noted, the sonic screwdriver has evolved substantially during the series aired so far. More interesting is the social commentary on the attitudes toward gadgets and new technology in the 21st Century. In several stories, humans are eager to embrace a new technological device or development, even if they do not fully understand it, so long as it meets the needs of the time. The David Tenannt-era two-parter 'The Sontaran Stratagem' / 'The Poison Sky' clearly demonstrates this theme. In this story, former companion Martha Jones, now with UNIT, phones up the Doctor and asks him to come back to Earth to investigate a remarkable new invention by Luke Rattigan, a brilliant teenager. This device, the Atmospheric Omission System, or ATMOS, is supposed to reduce carbon dioxide emissions from cars to zero, a fact that UNIT finds suspicious but is unable to prove is sinister. The device later turns out to be the invention of the monstrous Sontarans, who use Rattigan's ego as a manipulative tool to get him to distribute it. It is actually a means of releasing 'clone feed' into Earth's atmosphere and thereby converting it into a Sontaran cloning world. At this level, the story is pretty standard *Doctor Who* fodder. What is remarkable is that according to data from the story, ATMOS is installed on 400 million vehicles around the world.

While no clear timeline for the deployment of ATMOS is ever given, that level of market penetration is stunning. As one measure of comparison, in the five years after the launch of the remarkably successful iPhone, Apple reported 250 million had been sold worldwide.[51] Given the ATMOS device's remarkable success, it is hard not to see this as a comment on the early 21st

---

[51] Jordan Kahn. 'Five years after launch: Apple sold 250M iPhones, accounting for $150B in revenue.' *9to5 Mac*, 27 June, 2012, accessed 5 March 2014. http://9to5mac.com/2012/06/27/5-years-after-launch-apple-has-sold-250-million-iphones-accounting-for-150b-in-revenue/

Century's willingness to rush headlong into the next gadget phase, whether that be Facebook, Twitter or Flappy Bird. It is implied, if not expressly stated, in 'The Sontaran Stratagem' that people installed 400 million units of poorly-understood technology on their vehicles, including all British government ones, without ever considering that there might be a negative aspect to it. While it might strain credibility that, in the story, not one official group or agency found the hidden gas nozzles on ATMOS, it is also true that through the 1950s governments allowed tobacco companies to promote smoking as a means of improving health. Human society has a remarkable capacity to accept almost anything as normal, including new technology, and adapt to it quickly.

The rapid spread of technology, and the complacency that comes with it, are explored further in the Matt Smith episode 'The Power of Three'. In this story, myriad small boxes suddenly appear all over the Earth, prompting the Doctor and his friends Amy and Rory to investigate them, only to find they are apparently benign. For almost a year, the boxes sit on Earth, harmless and immobile in pantries, office cubicles and dozens of other out-of-the-way places until, at a given moment, they spring to life, doing very odd things, such as spewing fire, firing lasers or playing a version of the 'Chicken Dance'. The force behind the cubes, referred to as the Shakri, is using all this seemingly random action to probe the most effective way of attacking humans, which turns out to be by inducing cardiac arrest. Naturally, everything turns out well in the end, but the complacency toward poorly-understood technology in the episode also serves as a reminder to viewers not to be too comfortable with, or count too much on, things they do not fully understand.

The widespread acceptance of what appears to be a benign product adds a new development to issues of gadgetry in the programme. No-one would doubt that the western world, and arguably most of the world, is a highly digital society today. Mobile phones are so ubiquitous now as to be virtually unnoticeable, and tablet devices can be commonly seen in restaurants, public transport, classrooms and living rooms. A walk down many city streets with a wi-fi locator will reveal dozens of prospective networks. We have embraced the technology to such a point that many cannot imagine life without it; which is precisely why society can be so vulnerable to an attack by or from within that technology. The technology has become as widespread, and ignored, as the cubes of the Shakri invasion. So long as the devices remain benign and passive, few people even notice them. But when a virus or a piece of malware does hit, few people are prepared for it either. This is not to say that someone will write a piece of malicious code that makes a mobile phone electrocute its user. The potential perils of technological gadgets in the 21st Century are more likely to be digital than physical;. But the threats are no less insidious than in *Doctor Who*, as recurrent stories in the news about data theft, malware and computer viruses make clear. 'The Power of Three' offers viewers a way to consider what can happen when something is so widespread that no-one notices it anymore, even if no-one understands exactly how it works.

A similar theme about understanding technology plays out in the earlier Matt Smith-era story 'Victory of Daleks'. Winston Churchill and the British army are so desperate to defeat the Luftwaffe during the Blitz of the Second World War that they don't ask too many questions about the true origins of the Dalek that is able to blast Nazi aircraft from the sky. Certainly, savvy viewers of *Doctor Who* would immediately recognise the Dalek as a threat, and perhaps even recognise the guise of the Dalek as a servant figure from the earlier second Doctor story 'The Power of the Daleks'. In both cases, the Daleks are willing to obey orders from the humans and profess loyalty, so long as providing obedient service meets their own needs. From a storytelling perspective, then, there is no thought at all but that the Daleks have some sinister motive at work, which only the Doctor can sort out. From a socio-technological perspective, though, 'Victory of the Daleks' raises questions about the willingness to apply a poorly-understood technology to solve an urgent problem, even if the long-term consequences are not clear, as with Dr Oppenheimer and the Manhattan Project that spawned four decades of the Cold War.

The story 'Boom Town', from the premiere series of the revived programme, highlights this societal concern about long-term consequences and a lack of understanding in a very local and poignant way. While the episode aired in 2005, the question it raises in a peripheral way has been asked for decades: how do people decide about the use of science or technology when almost no-one understands it? In the serial, the lone surviving Slitheen from a previous story has landed in Cardiff and is spearheading a plan to build a new power plant. The proposition is argued to be good for the economy and growth of Cardiff, and to provide a source of new jobs. A very small number of people have uncovered some technological concerns about the nature of the plant – which is actually designed to blow up a large part of the planet in order to provide a shockwave the Slitheen can use to ride out of the solar system and on toward new conquests. These people have vanished. Most of the story revolves around a moral choice the Doctor must make in how to deal with the Slitheen, but the issues around the power plant and the populace are far more interesting from a science and technology point of view.

In the story, the power plant/explosive device is being built in Cardiff, with a nuclear fuel source, but this serves only as an example. Nuclear power is seen as a sort of bogeyman by much of the western world, so for storyline purposes it allows the most drama; because, as noted before, when it fails, it fails in a spectacular and devastating way. But how many people, when asked, could really explain how nuclear power works? If the populace does not understand the technology of the project, how can they be expected to make an informed decision on it, other than with jingoistic slogans? A frighteningly large number of people are completely ignorant of even the most basic scientific and technological processes. Consider a recent study released by the National Science Academy in the US, which found that in response to a true-or-false question, fully one-quarter of Americans did not know that the Earth revolved around the

Sun.[52] When there is no scientific understanding of a project such as a new power plant, even a non-nuclear one, how do people make a decision about it? In place of understanding, jingoism becomes the basis for decisions that may have significant regional and even global implications; and if something does eventually go wrong, those at fault can say the people voted to approve the projects. One can hope, as seen in the story, that some scientist, or even savvy journalist, will understand the potential implications and catch on before it is too late, but this places a lot of trust in those scientists; and in the event that two scientists do not agree, again the public are left to decide which one to believe, based on simplifications and jingoist marketing.

A programme like *Doctor Who*, being so steeped in technology, opens the door for people to ask important questions about it, and provides at least a limited way to counter the risks of scientific ignorance by engaging the public directly in real science. Given the number of replica sonic screwdrivers available commercially, including one that serves as a working television remote, and countless cobbled-together jobs by more devoted fans, it is no surprise that when in 2012 a new method of surgery using ultrasonic waves to rotate an object was tested, the headline referenced *Doctor Who*.[53] In the same light, when scientists inadvertently discovered a means of using photons to interact with physical structures in a more forceful way, the news headline referred to a 'real lightsaber' from the *Star Wars* films.[54] In both cases, as with the current efforts by NASA in the US to develop the principles of a working warp drive with obligatory

---

[52] Samantha Grossman. '1 in 4 Americans Apparently Unaware the Earth Orbits the Sun' *Time*, 16 February 2014, accessed 19 April 2015. http://time.com/7809/1-in-4-americans-thinks-sun-orbits-earth/

[53] 'Dr Who's sonic screwdriver "invented" at Dundee University.' *BBC News*, 19 April 2012, accessed 9 March 2014. http://www.bbc.com/news/uk-scotland-17760077

[54] Melissa Locker. 'Scientists Finally Invent Real, Working Lightsabers.' *Time*, 1 October 2013, accessed 9 March 2014. http://newsfeed.time.com/2013/10/01/someone-finally-invented-real-working-lightsabers/

Star Trek allusions, the reference to science fiction media allows the non-scientific public at least some limited way to understand the technology and perhaps make a more informed decision about it.

Throughout the history of *Doctor Who*, the relationship between science, technology and its application in the world through devices and gadgetry has explored some of society's fears and hopes. As the functionality of real-world technology increased, so did that of different far-fetched gadgets in the programme. Through it all, there have always been deeper questions asked about whether or not a device is really understood, or whether or not a technology or discovery has really been thought through. Outside the programme, these questions come up as concerns about the real nature of the mobile phone, or whether or not the boffins in the lab really understand just exactly what the Large Hadron Collider is going to do when switched on. While it may not always be the intention of the scriptwriter to provoke such thoughts, at times it is unavoidable, and the value of a programme like *Doctor Who* is that viewers can consider the issues safely, even if the lust for technological gadgets makes them long for a genuine sonic screwdriver or vortex manipulator at the same time as they ask questions about the safety of such a device.

Evil and War

'Clara, be my pal. Tell me: am I a good man?' It seems like after more than fifty years on the television and two thousand years of life by his own admission (though his estimations of his age seem to vary between incarnations!), the Doctor should have figured out whether or not he is a good man. Certainly, earlier in his lives, the Doctor seems to have had a clear perspective on the matter, as during episode two of 'The Moonbase' in 1967, speaking of the Cybermen, he says, 'Evil is what I meant. There are some corners of the universe which have bred the most terrible things. Things which act against everything that we believe in. They must be fought.' Because *Doctor Who* has been around for over fifty years, the question of good and evil has evolved considerably, leading the Doctor of today to ask very different questions from the Doctor of 1967. That considerable length of air-time has provided *Doctor Who* a useful means of evaluating the role of warfare in a society, as well as a means of assessing the nature of good and evil.

Warfare is hardly unique to the later part of the 20th Century. However, there are things that distinguish the wars of that century from previous conflicts. While there is an inherent risk to generalisation, it is reasonable to say that the wars of the 19th Century were limited in scope if not in length. A state of war might technically engulf an entire region, but the actual battles were localised affairs and generally involved armed forces on the scale of several hundreds to a few thousand men, although there were exceptions. Over the course of the three-day Battle of Gettysburg during the American Civil War, there were over

EVIL AND WAR

51,000 total dead on both sides.[55] The wars of the 20th Century easily dwarf this casualty toll, though. As a means of comparison, consider that in the Battle of the Somme during the First World War, by end of the first day there had been more casualties than in the whole of the three days at Gettysburg, and by the end of the first month, ten times as many – and the battle lasted a total of three months.[56]

In addition to soaring casualty rates, the 20th Century saw the beginning of what has been termed 'total war', wherein the entire effort of a nation is devoted to the war effort. That vast outlay of industrial capacity, in terms not only of actual military armaments but also of food, clothing and other day-to-day supplies, had never been required before, nor had the number of men needed to fight in the trenches. Both the scale of destruction and the wide-ranging locations of battlefields were also far beyond those of any previous war. The total property damage from the First World War is difficult to estimate, but various war reparation plans imposed on Germany afterwards by the Treaty of Versailles totalled billions of German marks. The Second World War was even more globally devastating. If the death rate of the First World War was appallingly high, at least a majority of those killed were in the various militaries. In the Second World War, a good estimate for the total number of troop deaths is around 15 million, or close to twice those killed in the First World War. But a conservative estimate allows there were also some 45 million civilians killed, and in some regions the total may have been significantly under-reported.[57] It is nearly impossible to generate an accurate cost in currency for

---

[55] 'The Battle of Gettysburg: Statistics.' *U Army*, accessed 12 March 2014. http://www.army.mil/gettysburg/statistics/statistics.html

[56] John Keegan. *The First World War*. (New York: Vintage, 1998). 295-299.

[57] 'By the Numbers: Worldwide Deaths.'
National WWII Museum, accessed 12 March 2014. http://www.nationalww2museum.org/learn/education/for-students/ww2-history/ww2-by-the-numbers/world-wide-deaths.html

the damage done during the Second World War, but the United States' Marshall Plan to help rebuild afterwards paid out some $13.7 billion, and did not make any payments to the Soviet Union, which was devastated by the Nazi invasion.[58]

By the time *Doctor Who* premiered in 1963, the immediate after-effects of the Second World War had begun to fade. The children watching in the UK as William Hartnell's Doctor first faced off against the Daleks were part of the 'baby boom' that followed the war, and almost certainly knew or interacted with a veteran in some aspect of their lives. But Europe had achieved considerable progress toward rebuilding. London was not completely free of the marks from the Blitz, but the wounds were healing, even if the ghosts of the war still haunted the streets in the form of bullet holes in building façades and the occasional discovery of an unexploded shell or bomb. In short, the drive to get on with things in the wake of the Second World War had been quite successful on many fronts.

However, there was another legacy of the war that was not so easy to repair, and it left much deeper scars on the world than any mere bomb could: the use of atomic weaponry against Japan in 1945. For the first few years after the war, the threat of the continued use of atomic weapons seemed remote, and the Korean War concluded without this happening. However, in 1963, the threat of full-blown nuclear war seemed very real. With the launch of the Soviet satellite Sputnik I in 1957, the worry over a nuclear confrontation had risen markedly. These fears reached a frightening crescendo in October 1962 when the US and the Soviet Union faced off over the deployment of medium-range missiles in Cuba, a confrontation known as the Cuban Missile Crisis. The US defence forces were at a defence condition or DefCon 2, which meant they were 15 minutes away from deploying the national nuclear arsenal before Soviet

---

[58] 'Cooperation for Recovery: The Marshall Plan' *International Monetary Fund*, accessed 12 March 2014. http://www.imf.org/external/np/exr/center/mm/eng/mm_dr_03.htm

Premier Nikita Khrushchev offered an agreement.[59]

In the Cuban stand-off, as in the Second World War, there were clearly-defined moral boundaries. During the war, the enemy was obvious, and it was simply unquestionable that the Nazis and Imperial Japan had to be defeated for the good of the whole world. This ideology carried over into the early Cold War. The western world, embodied by the US and Europe, were the good guys, defenders of freedom and liberty, while the Soviet Bloc took on the role of the Nazis, tyrannical oppressors of people and their freedom, an embodiment of evil. The Cold War backdrop framing out good versus evil in classic *Doctor Who* was most directly embodied by one of the Doctor's most popular and enduring foes, the Daleks.

From the very start of their time in *Doctor Who*, the Daleks have been presented as a terribly war-like race. Further, when first introduced, it is strongly implied if not blatantly stated that they became what they are not just because of a war, but because of a nuclear war. The radiation levels on the planet Skaro, where the Doctor, Susan, Ian and Barbara land in the episode 'The Dead Planet', are remarkably high, although the travellers do not know it initially, as they fail to spot the reading on the TARDIS's radiation meter. More poignant than the Daleks, who are not revealed fully until the second episode, is the effect the creepy dead forest has on the travellers when they first disembark from the TARDIS. The trees are all crumbling to ashes, and even a fearsome-looking but unfortunate animal of some kind has been petrified where it stood. In the wake of the images from Hiroshima and Nagasaki after the atomic attack of the Second World War, where shadows were burned into walls and vast swathes of cities reduced to ash and rubble, the potential destructive effect that a full nuclear war could have not just on cities but on the whole world was directly made manifest in *Doctor Who*.

---

[59] Letter, Soviet Premier Nikita Khrushchev to President Kennedy, 26 October 1962 as reproduced in *Major Problems in American History Since 1945*. (Boston: Wadsworth), 2007, 144-147.

DAVID JOHNSON

There has been some discussion about whether or not the Daleks were intended to represent the Nazis as an ultimate evil. Partly this may be due to later developments in the Dalek storyline, such as the genetic engineering that takes place in 'Genesis of the Daleks' or the racial purity issue that comes out in various tales. It is important to realise that none of this was in place in 1963 when Terry Nation developed the original storyline. In fact, Nation himself intended the creatures to be a one-shot monster, writing their destruction into the end of the seven-part serial. These first Daleks, trapped in their metal city on Skaro, were certainly war-like, callous toward non-Daleks, and self-serving, but not the fully evil race they became in later serials.

But evil they did become; a straight, non-nuanced force of malevolence spreading across the *Doctor Who* universe. When the Daleks next appeared in *Doctor Who*, they had invaded the Earth, which resulted in an iconic image of Daleks on Westminster Bridge amid a deserted London. These Daleks were more ruthless than they had been previously, using biological weapons to decimate the Earth before invading it, turning some humans into Robomen directly under their control, and enslaving the rest in a plot to make the planet into a mobile base by replacing its core with a drive system. There was no question the Daleks had to be defeated, whatever the cost. The later 12-part serial 'The Daleks' Master Plan' served to reinforce this blatant evil, as the creatures planned to use a Time Destructor weapon as part of a plot to rule the whole universe. The evil of the Daleks was further emphasised in the lengthy serial when two companions of the Doctor, Katarina from ancient Troy and human space agent Sara Kingdom, were both killed during the course of the action.

A curious change came to the Daleks in 1967. In the serial 'The Evil of the Daleks', the Doctor succeeds in implanting into a Dalek programming system something called the human factor. The net result of this is a batch of 'good' Daleks, presumably with an ability to perform benevolent deeds instead of just exterminating things. The result is a Dalek civil war, which appears to destroy the race completely. In 1967, few in the western world would have advocated that there was such a thing as a 'good' Communist, so why now was there a 'good' Dalek? From a production point of view, the Daleks were going to be written out of the programme, as Terry Nation wanted to launch them in their own series. But evil is hard to sell alone, and must be defeated when it is confronted by good, according to most media tropes, so perhaps it is unsurprising that this project never reached fruition. From a social point of view, though, there was something else at work, a question that would manifest itself throughout the entire run of the programme, up to the present day: who were the good guys?

The 1960s saw crises in many areas that resulted in fundamental shifts in social culture across much of the western world. A discussion of all the different social trends could easily occupy volumes, but in the context of *Doctor Who* and the nature of evil and war, there is one especially relevant event, commonly referred to as the Vietnam War. While the UK was not involved militarily in the conflict, the effects of it could be seen and felt all across the social landscape on both sides of the Atlantic. When the US got involved in Vietnam, it was presented as a clear case of good versus evil again, despite the frustrating and unsatisfactory conclusion to the Korean War of the early 1950s. But by 1967, the year of 'The Evil of the Daleks', the picture was much murkier. Images of the Vietnam War broadcast on the evening news seemed to showed little difference between the actions of the 'good guys' and the 'bad guys'. Further, the cost of the war in both money and in human lives was rapidly increasing, and there was no sign the 'good guys' were winning, despite governmental assurances that they were.

In the contrast between government statements about the war and media footage from it lies the other crucial aspect of social and moral shift in the 1960s. As soldiers from the war returned, and began to protest against the brutality of the conflict, people on both sides of the Pond began to question whether or not any war was a worthy cause. Was the enemy that different from us? The protests manifested in various ways, more vocally and visibly in the US as anti-war rallies fused with the burgeoning counterculture movement. Still, it was hard to deny the existence in the UK as well of efforts focused on promoting peace, love and understanding. A climactic moment for these counterculture efforts was the so-called Summer of Love in 1968, in which students on both sides of the Atlantic rose up to question the authority of those who told them to obey, and instead asserted a right to a world of free love and peace. While no one in the Summer of Love was advocating that Daleks need love too, such a sentiment might not have been entirely out of place.

It was a pipe-dream, of course; in some cases quite literally, given the profusion of psychoactive drugs that ran through much of the counterculture movement. That movement had largely dissipated by 1971. But the peace theme would manifest itself quite directly when the Daleks finally did return to *Doctor Who* in 1972, a time when the Strategic Arms Limitation Treaty, or SALT, was very much on the minds of a great many people.[60] While by no means a perfect treaty, SALT I, as it would later be known, was a remarkable first attempt to limit the growth of nuclear arms in the world, and it offered hope to the global community that humankind might actually be capable of stepping away from the abyss of nuclear holocaust. The treaty was directly manifested, if not expressly named, in 'Day of the Daleks'. While much of the serial involves the Doctor facing off against Daleks and a new enemy known as the Ogrons that work as their servants, the background story features humans from the future attempting to sabotage a peace conference because allegedly one of the delegates destroyed the conference, provoking a global war that allowed the Daleks to sweep in and invade the Earth again. Given that the discussions for SALT took place from 1969 to 1972, the treaty would certainly have

---

[60] 'Strategic Arms Limitations Talks (SALT 1).'
US State Department, accessed 14 March, 2014. http://www.state.gov/www/global/arms/treaties/salt1.html

been a recurrent theme in the media during the writing and making of 'Day of the Daleks', and it's not hard to see the parallels between SALT and the hopes of the global peace conference in the serial. Further commentary, if a bit heavy handed, can be found in the closing lines of episode four, when the Doctor charges peace delegate Sir Reginald Styles with making certain the conference is successful, as he and his companion Jo have seen what will happen if it is not.

A new take on morality came in the highly popular serial 'Genesis of the Daleks', featuring Tom Baker's incarnation of the Doctor. In this, the Doctor and his companions Harry Sullivan and Sarah Jane Smith, played by Ian Marter and Elisabeth Sladen respectively, materialise on an obviously war-torn planet instead of back on a space station as they expected. The Time Lords have diverted them because the Dalek threat to the galaxy is growing too great, and so the Doctor is tasked with destroying them at the very time of their creation. As the Doctor and company attempt to find their way into a military bunker, the hazards they encounter mirror images of the First and Second World Wars, where trenches lined with soldiers in gas masks cut across the landscape – although in this case the soldiers are dead and propped up to give the appearance of robust defences. 'Even the dead have a part to play,' the Doctor grimly comments. Inside the bunker, the wartime references are more focused on the Second World War, as the military attitudes and to an extent even the uniforms echo those of Nazi Germany, which may explain some of the later comparisons between Daleks and Nazis.

The serial also introduces one of the most significant additions to the Dalek mythos since their debut, in the form of Davros, their creator. Davros is terribly crippled, and survives only because of life support systems built into his chair, which deliberately resembles the base of a Dalek. However, Davros is certainly a brilliant scientist, and through genetic experimentation has determined that his race, the Kaleds, is changing as a result of the interminable warfare. He has now sped up that process to produce the final life-form, and designed a casing to allow that life-form to be mobile: the origin point of the Dalek. While the addition of Davros is engaging, and he will feature in every Dalek story afterwards in the classic programme, as well as popping up for appearances in the revived programme, there is a more interesting moral issue the Doctor faces in terms of a commentary on warfare.

Near the end of the serial, it appears victory is at hand for those opposing Davros. The incubators of the Daleks are wired with explosives, and the Doctor stands with two bared wires at the ready. If he touches the wires together, the Daleks will be destroyed forever, removed from the universe. But he questions whether or not he has that right. 'To destroy the Daleks?' Sarah Jane questions his concern. 'You can't doubt it.' 'But I do', the Doctor replies. 'You see, some things could be better off with the Daleks.' The Doctor further cites how many worlds will become allies simply because of their shared fear of the Daleks, and discusses with Sarah Jane the morality of travelling back in time to kill a child who will grow up to be a despotic dictator – a possible nod again to Hitler and Nazi Germany. 'But if I kill, wipe out a whole intelligent life form, then I become like them. I'd be no better than the Daleks.' In the end, the Doctor is unable to bring himself to connect the wires. Later, though, a Dalek runs over the wire ends, triggering the explosion anyway; but the Dalek production line has already started by this point. As he and his companions leave Skaro, the Doctor admits that the explosion will only delay the Daleks, but comments again that from the evil of the Daleks will come some greater good.

Peter Capaldi's Doctor has to confront a similar scenario in the two-part opener to Series Nine of the revival, when his words in 'Genesis of the Daleks' come back to haunt him. In the episode 'The Magician's Apprentice', he finds himself on a battlefield, where a small child is surrounded by 'hand-mines' that suck victims into the earth. Only, this child turns out to be the young Davros himself, and the Doctor initially flees, leaving him apparently doomed. After a tense conversation with the adult Davros about the value of compassion, and having discovered that the Daleks' language banks recognise the concept of mercy, the Doctor realises he must go back and rescue the young boy, in order to implant in his psyche the idea of mercy, so that he can eventually pass it on to the Daleks.

The Doctor's moral dilemma in 'Genesis of the Daleks' illustrated a seismic shift both within *Doctor Who* and within society as a whole. Previous encounters with foes had seen the destruction of an entire planet full of Cybermen with no remorse, and the Doctor willingly leaving the last of the Cybermen trapped in ice tombs forever, ostensibly ending the race. Yet in 'Genesis of the Daleks', the Doctor is unwilling to take the necessary action to achieve the same result for the Daleks, despite their being a more formidable foe for much of the programme's history. Societally, there was a more nuanced view of the nature of conflict by the mid-1970s than there had been in the 1960s. Could those groups purporting to represent good truly be considered good if they engaged in the same kinds of actions as the supposed enemy did? The unsettling end to the Vietnam conflict, with no clear victory, and the murky politics of the Cold War left the world much less certain about the nature of evil, and the value of warfare, than it had ever been.

Both the fifth Doctor and the sixth had encounters with the Daleks, but these tales offered little new material from a social perspective. This is not to say there were not moral dilemmas posed for these versions of the Doctor. Peter Davison's Doctor certainly agonises over the deaths of the Silurians and the Sea Devils in 'Warriors of the Deep', aware of the fact that while the humans view them as evil, these are ancient races that have just as much right to survive. And in 'The Trial of a Time Lord', Colin Baker's Doctor accuses the Time Lords of being corrupt, perhaps echoing the rising distrust of the government that began in the 1960s but was surely not improved by the Watergate scandal in the US, wherein President Nixon was called out for corruption charges relating to a criminal break-in attempt, while his Vice President, Spiro Agnew, was under federal investigation for corruption. But 1988's 'Remembrance of the Daleks' offers something quite different.

This sole encounter between Sylvester McCoy's Doctor and the Daleks is something new indeed. The Doctor's darker side begins to come out as he again confronts Davros and his Daleks, now engaged in an open conflict with another faction, the imperial Daleks. At the heart of the matter lies the Hand of Omega, a super-weapon capable of immense destruction. In the serial, the Doctor engages in almost Machiavellian schemes to ensure that the 'right' set of Daleks gets the Hand of Omega. In this case, the 'right' side is the group led by Davros; and once Davros has the weapon, the Doctor deliberately goads him into using it. The result is the complete destruction of Skaro, as the Doctor has pre-programmed the coordinates. This is a very different Doctor from the one who agonises over whether or not he has the right to destroy the Daleks in 'Genesis of the Daleks', and much closer to the one who asks whether or not he is a good man in 2014. It could be argued that the Doctor knew there were other Daleks still outside of Skaro, and so his actions would not result in the total elimination of the race, but the fact remains that the destruction of an entire planet of sentient beings must be seen as genocide – even if the revived programme has largely ignored this event since.

The events of 'Remembrance of the Daleks' can largely be seen in the context of yet another moral shift that took place during the late 1970s and 1980s. These decades saw the rise of a sort of 'ends justify the means' mentality that manifested itself in various banking and business scandals, the invasion of Grenada for no apparent reason by the US, illegal arms trades under President Ronald Reagan, and even the Argentinean invasion of the Falkland Islands, undertaken as an effort to distract the populace from internal problems in Argentina. The result was a period of time in which the question was no longer whether an action was right or wrong, but whether or not the perpetrator could get away with it and make things look good in the end. A noteworthy example is the mixed reaction to Lieutenant Oliver North during the Congressional hearings about the American arms scandal, with many seeing his willingness to work outside the rules in order to get the job done as an heroic trait rather than a violation of the law. In this context, the destruction of Skaro presents a darker, morally ambiguous Doctor who acts according to an ethical compass that is not so clearly subdivided into realms of right and wrong. Even the Doctor's companion Ace, at the end of the Dalek story, comments on this, wondering whether or not the Doctor's actions were 'good'. The Doctor is morally ambiguous in his reply, suggesting only, 'Time will tell.'

The world that *Doctor Who* finished broadcasting to in 1989 was still a Cold War world. If there were questions of moral ambiguity around the actions of individuals, the power structure was still very clear, as the western world, embodied by NATO, faced off against a clearly-defined foe in the Warsaw Pact and the Soviet Bloc. How quickly that changed! The opening of the Berlin Wall in November 1989 and the dissolution of the Soviet Union in 1991 marked a fundamental shift in the way the world operated. Suddenly the prospect of a century-long Cold War implied by 'Warriors of the Deep' was replaced by a 'New World Order' that is still being sorted in 2016. The question of good guys and bad guys, of a moral war, was uncomfortably explored in 1991 with the first Gulf War, commonly referred to as Operation: Desert Storm. The allied forces from many western nations were supposed to be the good guys, personified by General Norman Schwarzkopf. General Schwarzkopf gave media briefings akin to sports commentary, as video footage of 'smart bombs' hitting precision targets during the air war ran on television. The brief, 100-hour long land war seemed to indicate that this was a simple 'good versus evil' war again, and good was clearly going to triumph. However, as footage of the destruction on the ground and the oil fields on fire showed the true extent of the devastation, and the prospect of primary target Saddam Hussein remaining in power was manifesting itself, the question of a clear victory was much harder to answer.

Later events served only to muddle further the morality questions the world faced. The continued conflict in the Middle East, the terrorist attack on the US in 2001 and the resulting 'war on terror' that continues in 2016, mass transit attacks such as the London Tube bombing in 2005, and the rise of extremist forces all across the world, left deep and profound questions unanswered. What would be the cost of safety? Is it morally acceptable to use immoral or illegal methods to save countless lives? How far is too far?

This was very much the context the Doctor found himself in when the programme returned to BBC One in 2005. From the very start of the new stories, the Doctor makes it clear there has been a great Time War, a horrific conflict that has disrupted whole sections of the space-time continuum. Initially he seems to be his usual self, trying to put right what was made wrong by the Time War. But in the fourth episode, 'Dalek', he makes a shocking confession about the end of the conflict. 'Ten million ships on fire. The entire Dalek race wiped out in one second.' The single surviving Dalek accuses the Doctor of lying, to which he responds, 'I watched it happen. I made it happen!' The Doctor then admits that all the Time Lords burned with the Daleks, that 'Everyone lost.'

This moment marks a critical change in *Doctor Who*, a direct manifestation of the post-Cold War world. The Doctor, the traditional 'good guy' who always comes to the rescue, admits to nothing less than war crimes, to double genocide. The moral conundrum of being one of the 'good guys' who has also been guilty of horrific actions in the name of a greater good provides much of the background for the first eight series of the revived programme, ultimately leading to that question from Peter Capaldi's twelfth Doctor, 'Am I a good man?' In a way, the revived programme up to 2016 has been all about the moral redemption of the Doctor, and perhaps of society as a whole.

Many threads are woven into the complex tapestry of the programme since 2005. When a vast Dalek fleet threatens the Earth in the first-series finale 'The Parting of the Ways', the fact that the Doctor refuses to choose a genocidal solution again is a step toward redemption. This does not mean that the Daleks escape, though. The 'Bad Wolf' version of Rose, empowered by energy from the time vortex, steps in and herself commits genocide against the Daleks, dividing their individual molecules and spreading them across space. The Daleks still represent an ultimate evil, so viewers feel no sympathy for their destruction, but the fact remains that there is no debate about whether or not Rose, or the Doctor, has any right to obliterate a sentient race. If a sentient race or being is a threat to everything a person believes in, and will destroy that person and that belief system, then destruction is a rational necessity, isn't it? This line of thinking resonates well with extremists all across the world of 2016, from jihadists in the Middle East to militant anti-Obama conservatives in the US.

Other moments explore the moral conundrum the Doctor, and the viewers, have faced. During 'The Christmas Invasion', the Doctor confronts and neutralises a threatened alien invasion, but an early version of the Torchwood group promptly fires a high-powered weapon that destroys the enemy ship. This prompts sharp criticism from the Doctor, yet he himself routinely blows up spacecraft, as in the later Christmas special 'The Doctor, the Widow and the Wardrobe', or more poignantly when he obliterates an entire Cyberman fleet as part of 'A Good Man Goes to War' to send 'a message' to the Cybermen. Granted, the Cybermen are an established 'evil' in the programme, but the same sort of moral questions about the right to destroy a sentient race must come up on some level.

Davros directly points out how complex the moral interplay is in the Dalek-centric finale to Series Four of the revived programme, 'Journey's End'. The Doctor, aided by a cadre of companions including Captain Jack Harkness, Sarah Jane Smith, Rose Tyler and a humanised clone of himself, faces off against Davros and his Daleks. Noting the homicidal and even genocidal tendencies of all of his companions, Davros says to the Doctor, 'I created the Daleks, Doctor, but you created this.' Further, the Doctor is aghast when his humanised clone overloads the power running into the Dalek fleet and blast it to ashes, even though he himself willingly committed genocide on a much larger scale during the Time War. The contrast in action and reaction highlights the complex morality that the 21st

Century faces on a regular basis, as well as demonstrating the way the programme has morally evolved over time.

As a central plot thread in the revived programme, many episodes either reference the Time War or the actions the Doctor took during it, but the fiftieth anniversary cycle of stories serves as a means to redefine the morality of *Doctor Who* more than any prior to that point. The episode 'The Name of the Doctor', the mini-episode 'The Night of the Doctor', the fiftieth anniversary feature 'The Day of the Doctor' and the 2013 Christmas special 'The Time of the Doctor' solidify the programme's new efforts to confront the moral complexity of the 21st Century world, both within its own plot structure and for the society watching it.

In 'The Name of the Doctor', the Doctor and Clara wind up on the planet Trenzalore, once again confronting the Great Intelligence. Near the climax, there is a poignant scene that definitively underscores the nuanced and complex perceptions of morality and warfare in *Doctor Who*. The physical embodiment of the ethereal Great Intelligence addresses the actions the Doctor has taken over his many lives, and calls him 'the cruel tyrant' and 'the slaughterer of ten billion'. Nowhere in the revived programme is there a more direct manifestation of 21st Century perceptions of war and the costs that come with it. By 2013, there was an implicit recognition in the western world that the casualties of war, any war, are humans. No matter how urgent the need for armed confrontation is, no matter how just the political or moral cause, the good guys and the enemy are both going to suffer, and the very notion of good and evil is largely subject to where a person stands on a battlefield, or in a war room. From the point of view of the various enemies – the Daleks, Cybermen, Sontarans, Rutans, Slitheen, Zygons and a hundred other races – the Doctor is the 'bad guy', the force opposing the assertion of whatever right or goal the opposing race wishes to defend or create.

Within this new moral compass of *Doctor Who*, executive producer Steven Moffat felt the need to address the programme's biggest moral issue: the Time War, and the

Doctor's genocidal role in it. To do that, he had to do some remarkable retro-continuity work in 'The Name of the Doctor'. At the story's climax, as the Doctor leaps into his own timestream to save Clara from dissipation within it, he confronts his great secret, a mysterious figure played by John Hurt, who is introduced in the closing credits as 'The Doctor'. This previously unseen Doctor is visible on a rocky cliff overlooking a scene of fire and presumed destruction, which, in light of later revelations, viewers can now assume was Gallifrey during the Time War.

The mini-episode noted before, 'The Night of the Doctor', provides some further clarification for viewers, as well as offering a nice surprise by explaining how the eighth Doctor, as played by Paul McGann in the 1996 TV movie and numerous audio adventures since, regenerates into this new Doctor. In the brief story, it is clear the Time War has been going for some time, and Paul McGann's version of the Doctor has been doing what he can, but not as a combatant. When the woman the Doctor is trying to save refuses to board the TARDIS, expressing her disgust at the Time Lords for the widespread destruction in the universe, the Doctor crashes with her and her ship rather than flee; but he just happens to crash on Karn, where – as noted previously – the Sisterhood of the Eternal Flame awaits him. They give him the means to regenerate, despite his having died in the crash, and offer him the power to choose whatever he needs. With his last words, the eighth Doctor chooses 'warrior', and thus regenerates into John Hurt's version of the Doctor, referred to in the closing credits of the mini-episode as 'The War Doctor'.

While the addition of the War Doctor to the *Doctor Who* canon gave many fans a moderate conniption in terms of the numbering of the Doctors in the revived programme, it also allowed Steven Moffat to settle for himself and possibly for *Doctor Who* fandom the question of the Doctor and the Time War. At the crux of the matter is the same basic question as in 'The Name of the Doctor' and in 21st Century perceptions of warfare in general: are there good guys in a war? The means to answer this in *Doctor Who* involved understanding how the Doctor could make the decision to destroy billions and billions of sentient life-forms 'in the name of peace and sanity', as the War Doctor protests when viewers first see him.

The introduction of the War Doctor is not the first exploration of the problem, certainly. In David Tenannt's send-off story, 'The End of Time', viewers learned two disturbing pieces of news about the Time War. The first was that the Doctor's long-time enemy, the Master, was driven to his nefarious actions by the High Council of the Time Lords, who planted a rhythmic code in his brain as a child to allow them a means of escaping the time lock that shuttered the Time War away from the rest of the universe at its conclusion. This certainly gives pause to considering the Time Lords as morally good. However, the second revelation is more critical in making them appear genuinely reprehensible. The High Council, led by Rassilon as played by Timothy Dalton, was willing to destroy the entire universe in order to end the Time War and allow only the Time Lord race to transcend onto a higher plane of existence. The Doctor claims that, given this information, he had no choice, and that he had to stop them at whatever cost. In this context, despite the fact that the Doctor did destroy Gallifrey, he did so to save the rest of the universe. While this may allow the War Doctor to be a 'good guy' in one sense, acting in the name of peace and sanity as he asserts, the argument that the ends justify the means, that the deaths of billions is an appropriate exchange for the lives of hundreds of billions, may be a hard argument to accept if not all those billions are necessarily evil, and in some cases are in fact children, as becomes clear in 'The Day of the Doctor'.

In 'The Day of the Doctor', viewers are taken further into the Time War than ever before. The war is at a critical point. The Daleks have finally breached Gallifreyan defences, and Gallifrey's second city has fallen. Driven by this change of events, the War Doctor breaks into a high security archive and steals the Moment, a sentient super-weapon that can end the war. Much of the story interaction between the Doctors is driven by the Moment's visual interface, embodied by the Bad Wolf version of Rose Tyler from Christopher Eccleston's final story. Rose manipulates time to allow the War Doctor a chance to see what he will become if he engages the weapon and destroys Gallifrey. Having seen this, though, he still opts to fire the weapon, despite knowing the costs, and that a later version of himself will count all the dead children he created by his decision; that he will become 'the man who regrets' in David Tenannt's Doctor, and 'the man who forgets' in Matt Smith's.

Just as the War Doctor is about to engage the Moment, though, two TARDISes materialise. Fresh from facing a very similar situation on Earth, where UNIT commander Kate Stewart, daughter of Brigadier Lethbridge-Stewart, was willing to destroy London to save the planet, the tenth and eleventh Doctors step out, willing to push the big red button with the War Doctor, so that he doesn't have to make the choice alone. However, with prompting from Clara, Matt Smith's Doctor changes his mind, saying that he has 'had four hundred years to think about this' and has come up with a new plan. With help from every incarnation of the Doctor known, including a cameo by twelfth Doctor Peter Capaldi, whose casting was announced shortly before the fiftieth anniversary special aired, Gallifrey is shifted into a 'pocket universe' from where it can be later rescued, when things are safe again. In this solution, the Daleks destroy themselves, rather than being destroyed by the Doctor, as all the firepower they had been directing at Gallifrey passes through the now empty space the planet previously occupied, striking and destroying the 'billion billion' Daleks that had been orbiting and besieging it. This would seem to be much closer to the events of 'Remembrance of the Daleks', in which the Doctor does not actually destroy Skaro himself, but instead goads Davros into doing so. While this frees the Doctor from the direct genocidal actions that have been weighing on him since the revived programme premiered, it is still in enough of a moral grey area to require further consideration.

The finale of Matt Smith's era in 'The Time of the Doctor' frames the question that will drive much of Peter Capaldi's first series, and also the evaluation that the world of 2016 still struggles with morally. In the story, the Doctor returns again to Trenzalore, where an endless war is taking place, potentially the last battle of the Time War, as the rescued Gallifrey from 'The Day of the Doctor' has been sending out a signal, effectively asking if it is safe to come back. Hundreds of races fear the return of the Time Lords, and so engage in a lengthy siege of Trenzalore in order to prevent it, trapping the Doctor there. The Doctor devotes his time for hundreds of years to defending the small town of Christmas, trying to be a good man before facing his own death of old age. Just as the Doctor is dying, however, the Time Lords send him a new cycle of regeneration energy. While previously in the revived programme the Doctor's regenerations have become progressively more energetic, with some resulting destruction, this one takes on an epic scope, as the Doctor almost gleefully directs massive amounts of his own regeneration outflow toward the Dalek spaceship, even taunting his enemies with the phrase 'Love from Gallifrey' as it is obliterated. While viewers knew the Doctor would be victorious, as the next Doctor had already been cast and had even made a cameo appearance in the programme, the question remains: is the gleeful destruction of an enemy a suitable action for the 'good guys' to take?

Thus, the question from all of this is, 'Am I a good man?' Can a good man go to war, and come back unchanged? Much of Series Eight explores that very theme in complex ways. The Doctor must confront his own darkness in 'Into the Dalek', where, in an effort to understand why one Dalek is suddenly 'good', he and Clara miniaturise themselves and go inside it. The Doctor repairs a radiation breach, at which point the Dalek reverts to its exterminating nature. Clara, however, forces the Doctor to consider a way to make the Dalek good again. So, while she attempts to unlock good memories from its data banks, the Doctor plugs himself into its brain and tries to give it 'something amazing'. In other words, the Doctor tries to show the Dalek amazing things from his travels. However, the Dalek latches onto the deep hatred the Doctor has for the Daleks, and images from the Time War. In the end, the Doctor must try to come to terms with the statement from the Dalek, 'I am not a good Dalek. You are a good Dalek.' This would certainly seem to answer the question about whether or not the Doctor is a good man; but, as with much of life in 2016, things are not so simple.

Clara's boyfriend Danny Pink, a new semi-regular in Series Eight, serves as a means of exploring this question further, and of forcing the Doctor to do so as well. It is established that Danny was a soldier serving in the Middle East, where he accidentally killed a boy as part of a mission. He is clearly traumatised by this event, although he never speaks of it to anyone until Clara finally learns the truth in the climactic story 'Death in Heaven'. Danny has tried very hard to lead a normal life, teaching at Coal Hill School and attempting to make a relationship with Clara, despite her diverse adventures. But, in the end, Danny is too aware of what his actions cost him, and when in 'Death in Heaven' he is given the chance to redeem those actions by saving the boy he killed, reviving him from the Nethersphere, he opts to so do, even though it costs him his own life and the chance to be with Clara again.

Danny is also the means by which the Doctor is finally able to answer his own question, 'Am I a good man?' The plot of 'Death in Heaven' is complex and involves the return of the Master, in the form of Missy, and the Cybermen. Danny is made into a Cyberman, but elects not to complete the conversion process by activating the emotional inhibitor. In the climactic moment, set in a graveyard, Missy appears and grants the Doctor full control of the new Cyberman army, saying he can use it to fix the wrongs of the universe. 'Armies are for people who think they're right. And nobody thinks they're righter than you,' she tells him. The moral crisis the Doctor has been facing for the entire revival of the programme now comes to a head. Is it possible for a good man to do what the Doctor has done? Can the Doctor, or Danny Pink, or anyone, go to war and not come back changed?

'I am not a good man', the Doctor finally decides. 'I am not a bad man. I am not a hero. And I'm definitely not a president. And no, I'm not an officer. Do you know what I am? I am an idiot, with a box and a screwdriver. Just passing through, helping out, learning.' The Doctor, like the viewers, must face up to an increasingly complex set of moral choices and issues, including the use of war in the name of peace. He, and they, are forced to realise that he just keeps muddling through with the best moral compass he can manage, trying to do the right thing in a world where the right thing is no longer always clear and obvious.

Doctor Who of the 1960s allowed for an exploration of nuclear fears, complete with utterly ruined and destroyed worlds. The 1960s era of the programme also allowed a recognition that there are evil forces in the universe and that 'they must be fought'. The enemies were unrepentantly evil, and should be fought with any means necessary. In the 1970s, *Doctor Who* manifested the social shift of the time, a shift that saw war as inevitably having consequences, and an acknowledgement that even in unrestrained warfare, it was necessary not to commit atrocities simply in the name of victory. The 1980s saw *Doctor Who* acknowledge the continuing threat of the Cold War, even as there was hope that it would not become a 'hot war', as there can be no winners in such a war, or possibly in any war. With the revived programme, the exploration of war has focused more on the costs, the consequences and the desire to find a better way, even if the odds are tremendously against it. This is not to say *Doctor Who* will not feature warfare again, or even large-scale destruction of 'bad guys'. But if the programme is any indicator, the world of 2016 may not be able wholly to condone the use of violence as a means to solve problems, as most recently and strikingly affirmed by the conclusion of 'The Zygon Inversion'. As the line between good guys and bad guys continues to blur, both the society watching *Doctor Who* and the Doctor himself will have to continue to make the best possible choices at the time, which is all anyone can ever hope to do.

DAVID JOHNSON

The Future of Humanity

Doctor Who is and always has been an inherently hopeful programme. Week after week, even when things seem at their darkest, the Doctor always manages to save the day, the world and at times the whole universe. This has even become somewhat self-referential in the revived programme, as on several occasions the Doctor uses his own record as a means of saving the day yet again, most notably in 'Forest of the Dead', where he intimidates the Vashta Nerada by telling them to look him up in the Library, and in 'The Eleventh Hour', when he threatens the Atraxi with the statement, 'Hello. I'm the Doctor. Basically, run.' There can be little doubt that no matter how grim the situation appears, 'The Doctor will save me', as UNIT operative and apparent fangirl Osgood says over and over in 'The Day of the Doctor'. But there is an entirely different level on which *Doctor Who* is a hopeful programme, found in the repeated assertion that humanity has great potential; that it will not just survive, but will have a great destiny in the universe, leaving a profound and indelible mark.

Modern humanity's sense of itself in the universe can be traced back to developments in the Renaissance and the period known as the Enlightenment. Early scientists like Galileo and Christian Huygens opened up vast new worlds, and demonstrated that the Earth was but one of many planets in an amazing universe. Writers like John Locke, Thomas Hobbes and Jean Jacques Rousseau defined the principles by which modern society operates, or at least, would like to operate. There was an acknowledgement of basic human rights such as life, liberty and the pursuit of property, and the formalisation of the social contract that says in a civilised world everyone gives up certain rights, such as the right to do an action simply because the individual has the strength to do so, but that in return for the giving up those few rights, the government of a society guarantees myriad others. There was even an open admission that the society of this era, the 17th and early 18th Centuries, was not yet an Enlightened age, but an era of Enlightenment, where humanity was moving toward its potential.

Three hundred-odd years later, one wonders what a reassessment from Locke or Rousseau would produce. Certainly, there has been some degree of progress. In the wake of the Second World War, there was a marked shift in much of Western Europe. There was a recognition among many governments, including the UK's, that things could not go back to the way they were before the war. A greater set of social safety-nets was needed to mitigate the worst effects of poverty and ill health. The economic prosperity in the US, and its Marshall Plan that helped rebuild war-torn nations, also played a role, as the National Health Service was introduced and a more robust benefit system developed. Was this to be the Enlightened society, finally?

That question was very difficult to answer when *Doctor Who* premiered in 1963, and the task got only more challenging as the decade wore on. The 1960s was marked by great conflict and great triumph, by violence and marches for peace, and a human race that went looking into outer space as well as the inner mind. It was the decade of the first manned landing on the Moon and a violent series of political assassinations, including that of John F Kennedy, the man who had proposed to send US astronauts to make that landing. It was the decade that saw the rise of a counterculture of free love as well as the rise of the Berlin Wall, dividing East from West for more than forty years. It was the decade that saw thousands die in the swamps and jungles of Vietnam even as robotic emissaries of humanity explored vast new worlds in our solar system. It was not the Utopia Sir Thomas Moore had written about in the Renaissance, but there was still hope mankind might find its way there, out among the stars. This was the decade in which *Doctor Who* began.

The serials of the programme's early years offer no great

insights individually, but collectively they give a distinct picture of how humanity was progressing at that time, particularly in regards to space. William Hartnell's tenure as the Doctor did not generally address human space travel or humanity's future, but instead involved adventures on other planets where humanoid aliens lived. A rare exception is 'The Daleks' Master Plan', in which there is a notable human presence in space around the year 4000. Humans are represented by Space Security Service (SSS) agents Brett Vyon, as played by Nicholas Courtney (later to become Brigadier Lethbridge-Stewart), and Sara Kingdom, as played by Jean Marsh. What the exact nature of these agents is, as well as the overall nature of Earth's involvement in the galaxy, is not made expressly clear, but it is apparent that humanity is determined to stop the Daleks and preserve its own solar system.

With Hartnell's farewell serial, 'The Tenth Planet', though, a bright future history began to take shape. In this 1966 serial, viewers got a glimpse at Earth twenty years into the future, as the story was set in 1986. In this version of 1986, space flight is a commonplace event, with multiple spacecraft being placed in peril by the arrival of rogue planet Mondas. Further, it is noted at one point that a flight to the Moon has just returned; an apparently regular occurrence for 1986. Given the apparent rapid progress humans were making with spaceflight in 1966, it seemed plausible that in twenty years' time flying into space would be no more difficult than early air travel had been. Worth noting in this future is that the space capsules represented in the story are still two-seat models, closely mirroring the NASA Gemini craft that were flying in 1965 and 1966, although much roomier than them. There is no evidence of a three-seat spacecraft, despite the three-seat capsule of NASA's Apollo programme being well into the development phase by 1966, having completed more than one test flight.[61] This may be a

---

[61] 'Apollo Flight Tests' *NASA*, 1968, accessed 24 March 2014. http://www.hq.nasa.gov/alsj/CSM05_Apollo_Flt_Tests_pp33-38.pdf pp. 33-38.

narrative conceit, in as much as a third astronaut might have been unnecessary or even cumbersome from a writing point of view, but it also represents what the public expected in a spacecraft, based on the images coming from orbit on a regular basis. The core assumption in the serial, though, was that humankind would continue to make steady progress toward a brighter future off-world.

With the Patrick Troughton era in the TARDIS, there is a general move toward more humans being seen in space; a widespread presence that is almost taken for granted. The second Doctor's first adventure, 'The Power of the Daleks', is set on the distant planet Vulcan, but features a very human base, and a very human story about power and bureaucracy, with the Daleks simply serving as a convenient threat and a guarantee of viewership for the radical change that *Doctor Who* went through with that first regeneration. More directly, though, it is not treated as being at all unexpected that humans have colonised a distant world. Even relatively new companions Ben and Polly seem unsurprised that humans have reached out into the galaxy. When the Doctor and his friends land outside a Moonbase in the year 2070 a few episodes later, there is no surprise – except perhaps from newcomer Jamie, an 18th Century Scottish piper – that humans have by this point colonised the Moon and taken control of the weather through technology, despite the fact that when 'The Moonbase' was first broadcast, humans had not yet set foot on the Moon. Many other stories from the Patrick Troughton run feature humans in various times and places throughout the galaxy, such as landing on Telos around the 25th Century in 'Tomb of the Cybermen' or running a giant space station in 'The Wheel in Space'. In each story, it is simply accepted that humans will colonise space, that the technology will evolve and humans will move out into the universe just as they moved across the face of the Earth. *Doctor Who* of the 1960s presented viewers with a bright, gleaming future of high-tech equipment and ultramodern designs, shiny bases and spacecraft where humans could sit at computer consoles and run the entire system with the push of a button.

That bright future began to dim a little in the 1970s, although not right away. Five additional missions to the Moon took place in the early 1970s, and it seemed likely that humans could reach Mars by the 1980s. It was no surprise, then, that when Jon Pertwee's Doctor found himself stranded on an Earth roughly contemporaneous to that of the viewing audience, there would be a mission to Mars under way in the serial 'The Ambassadors of Death'. This mission, known as Mars Probe 7, is obviously not unique, although it is unclear if there have actually been as many as six flights previously. But when the mission runs into trouble, a Rescue 7 mission is quickly put together, reaffirming that human interplanetary travel is common and easily achieved. The story itself, a commentary on xenophobia, is not especially remarkable, but in the context of earlier continuity from the programme, serves to affirm the belief from the 1960s and 1970s that humans were destined to travel to the planets and the stars.

While Jon Pertwee spent his first few serials officially marooned on Earth, the Time Lords were not above using him for special missions, as in 'Colony in Space'. This 1971 serial is remarkable both as the first to show the Doctor visiting another world since *Doctor Who* made the transition from black-and-white to colour production in 1970, and as the first to indicate that space travel might not be as easy as it had previously appeared. The story involves the Master and a doomsday weapon, but the backdrop is more instructive, as it features an agrarian colony coming up against a powerful Interplanetary Mining Corporation (IMC). The farmers on the planet Uxarieus left the Earth due to overcrowding, pollution and a callous bureaucracy, but now struggle with less-than-perfect equipment and the oppressive power of the IMC. Near the climax, after the IMC engineer has certified that the colony spacecraft is safe, we see it take off and explode, presumably killing all the colonists. While things work out well in the end, and all bar one of the colonists are revealed to have escaped before the explosion, the crucial new presentation is that the future of humankind in space might not be as rosy and perfect as it had been thought to be.

THE FUTURE OF HUMANITY

While other Jon Pertwee-era serials continued to comment on humanity's fate in the universe, they added little to what had gone before, and generally focused around the medium-term future of humankind, not venturing much past the year 3000. However, the clock shifted dramatically forward in the second story of Tom Baker's tenure, 'The Ark in Space', in which the TARDIS materialises in a very distant future. While the year is never directly established, it is one of the farthest futures seen to this point in *Doctor Who*. The Doctor notes that some of the technology of the Ark – in fact a space-station called Nerva – seems to date from the 30th Century; but the humans on board were set to sleep for 5,000 years, and have actually 'overslept' by a significant amount of time. Thus viewers are left to wonder how many untold centuries into the future the story is actually set, although the figure of 10,000 years is bandied about. The technology visible here is not much different from other 1970s perceptions of what a future should look like, with large consoles of equipment and generally gleaming white rooms and corridors. The humans went into the Ark because of the risk of massive solar flares that would destroy most life on Earth; a premise apparently borne out by the surface conditions seen in the following story, 'The Sontaran Experiment'. With 'The Ark in Space', *Doctor Who*'s commentary regarding human potential broaches a new subject: not only how far humans will reach into the universe, but how long they will endure. In this particular serial, the affirmation is that humans could manage to endure an 'extinction event' and come back to Earth to repopulate the planet; presumably a better planet, as the Ark's occupants were selected to give the best chance of survival.

There is a potentially sinister implication to 'The Ark in Space', though, and it crops up again in more than one later example of distant-future humankind in *Doctor Who*. The term eugenics was coined at the turn of the 20th Century, and with it came the misapplication of the idea of Darwinian evolution to suggest that the 'best' of humanity needed to preserve its genes against dilution or contamination from the lesser classes – primarily the working class. The notion of asserting that any race was inherently dominant or superior to any other generally did not come up in polite or informed conversation after the Second World War, but by any other name, selecting the best of society still harks back to the central premise of eugenics, and that is exactly what has happened in 'The Ark in Space'. While not directly part of the narrative, a fair question to consider is whether those humans left behind on Earth to face the solar flares blithely accepted their fate, or whether they harboured any resentment toward the chosen few selected to save humanity and eventually rebuild the species. Equally so, when those who were to survive were placed into the Ark, did they give any thought to those left behind? The few people the Doctor does encounter during the course of the serial seem very driven, career-focused individuals who show little emotion. While humanity survives the extinction event – and we learn in the following story, 'The Sontaran Experiment', that some of those left behind also managed to escape and colonise other worlds – it is debatable what kind of society the survivors from the Ark would recreate on Earth.

In both the Jon Pertwee and the Tom Baker eras, it is possible to see the gradual disillusionment that society underwent during the 1970s. Mankind's explorations of space seemed to have stalled after the last lunar landing in 1972, and the era of peace and harmony, the 'Age of Aquarius' that companion Jo Grant refers to in the 1971 story 'The Dæmons', seemed also to have failed to take hold, as the counterculture movement faltered and a capitalistic society reasserted itself. There was also the first significant wave of ecological awareness that challenged the chemical industry and governmental regulations, and grassroots efforts like the first Earth Day in 1970. Instead of the gleaming-bright and outward-bound future envisioned in the 1960s, during the 1970s society generally turned inward, so much so that this is sometimes referred to as the 'me decade'. While the *Doctor Who* of this period never directly addressed the issue of an inward focus, the general tone of its depictions of humanity's future was more muted than the previous 1960s optimism.

THE FUTURE OF HUMANITY

The 1980s saw the popularisation of dystopian visions of mankind's future. These can be traced back to the Victorian era, when stories like *The Time Machine* by H G Wells and *After London* by Richard Jefferies showed the possibility of a less-than-perfect future world. But 1982 marked two major events that brought such imperfect futures to a much broader audience. The first was the release of the film *Blade Runner*, directed by Ridley Scott, in which a future Los Angeles is shown to be dilapidated and crime-ridden, such that all those who can afford to do so have moved to off-world colonies. The second event was the publication of the short story 'Burning Chrome' by William Gibson, which kicked off the subgenre of cyberpunk literature. If the future of the 1970s was dimmed from its earlier potential, the future that people of the 1980s saw was often disastrously bad.

Doctor Who came to reflect this dystopian future to a degree, most directly in the Peter Davison-era serial 'Frontios'. No date is ever specified for the TARDIS's arrival point here, but the action takes place sometime after the Earth has collided with the Sun, which could be anything up to five billion years from 1984, when the serial was broadcast. To escape destruction, at least some humans have set out across the galaxy in a giant ship, much like the earlier Ark. However, the ship has crash-landed on the planet Frontios as a result of malicious alien Tractators manipulating gravity, and the surviving humans seem almost helpless. They are dependent on giant glow-sticks for lighting, have trouble maintaining electrical power, and generally live more like Robinson Crusoe than a five-billion-year-old species that can travel the galaxy. The future of 'Frontios' is a far cry from the powerful human futures seen earlier, and suggests humanity may become more like interplanetary refugees than masters of the galaxy.

By the time *Doctor Who* went off the air for an extended period at the end of the 1980s, there was a growing awareness that the conquest of space was not going to be easy and that progress was much harder than expected. While it was not the first disaster in space exploration, the explosion of the space shuttle *Challenger* in 1986 demonstrated that spaceflight continued to be a risky business; a fact that was brutally reaffirmed with the disintegration of the space shuttle *Columbia* during its re-entry to Earth's atmosphere in 2003. In light of the apparently slow pace of progress and the very real risk of disaster, when *Doctor Who* relaunched in 2005, a new attitude was obvious.

In the programme, humans of the future are still spreading across the galaxy, to be certain. There are repeated references to different human galactic empires in various stories such as 'Planet of the Ood' and 'The Waters of Mars'. But this presentation of the future is different from the gleaming white sets of the 1970s and 1980s. In 'The Impossible Planet', for example, the planetary base on which the tenth Doctor and Rose find themselves seems more like a 21st Century industrial complex than a high-tech product of a space-conquering civilisation. Although it certainly features plenty of tech, it is grungy, spartan and hardly gleaming. Rose even comments on this, saying, 'It's funny, because people back home think that space travel's going to be all whizzing about and teleports and anti-gravity, but it's not, is it? It's tough.' This premise is reinforced in the serial '42', in which the Doctor and his new companion Martha find themselves stuck on a disabled and nearly decrepit space freighter as it drifts toward a star. Again, the ship seems more like an oil platform or an industrial plant than an interstellar spacecraft, with lots of exposed pipes, wiring running everywhere, dim lighting and general grunge. This aesthetic line, which can perhaps be traced back to the space freighter in another Ridley Scott-directed movie, 1979's 'Alien', is developed further through the revived programme in stories such as 'The Waters of Mars', 'The Beast Below', 'A Good Man Goes to War' and 'Journey to the Centre of the TARDIS', to name just a few. In each case, the future is not bright and gleaming, but is instead utilitarian, at times grungy, and often fraught with great peril. The only ships that actually seem like 'traditional' spaceships are the commercial liners featured in 'Voyage of the Damned', 'The Time of Angels' and 'The

Husbands of River Song', which are more akin to the *Queen Mary 2* than to the International Space Station, and so are expected to present a certain façade to their passengers and hide the deeper workings of the ship, which again point to a utilitarian and difficult future.

While the work required to achieve its future may be hard and risky, humanity does seem to have fantastic potential in the revived programme. The destruction of Earth mentioned in 'Frontios' is actually seen by the Doctor and Rose in the second story broadcast in 2005, 'The End of the World', where a central plot point focuses on the nature of what 'pure' humans are. Cassandra, the face of skin stretched over a frame, asserts that she is the last pure human, and that humanity has been diluted or modified by breeding with other species over the millennia. Certainly, there are some interesting-looking human-like creatures to be seen on the space station that serves as the story's setting, including the tree-human Jabe from the Forest of Cheem, who dies by fire while helping the Doctor save the rest of the observers watching the destruction of the Earth. But the humans on Frontios look quite like those of the 21st Century, suggesting that there may be many diverse lines of humanity that spread out across the galaxy or even galaxies over time.

Humans do indeed seem to have a lengthy future ahead of them. In the 2008 story 'Utopia', the Doctor and Martha land on a world at a time when the very universe itself is going out, the primal subatomic forces of matter finally failing. While largely theoretical in nature, current physics suggests this would be trillions of years from now, or almost unimaginably past the five-billion-year future setting of 'Frontios' and 'The End of the World'. Notably, some of the humans who are seeking Utopia in the eponymous story do have the kind of mixed features seen in 'The End of the World', but many others look no different from passengers on the London tube in 2016. But this is the great strength of humans, from 'The Ark in Space' to 'Utopia': they adapt to whatever conditions they find themselves in. That may be part of the reason why humans seem to have such potential in *Doctor Who*.

Adaptability is a very human trait, not necessarily in an evolutionary sense, but in terms of the day-to-day acceptance of what is normal. Curiosity is another common human trait, and one often projected into our creations, including Time Lords. These two traits are a powerful combination, and *Doctor Who* serves to remind us of what is possible for our species. As the Doctor comments before giving the human Zach a big hug in 'The Impossible Planet', 'Why did you come here? ... Because it was there ... Oh, human beings. You are amazing!' *Doctor Who* has provided an ongoing way for humankind to assess its own potential and future over the past fifty-odd years, from the bright and adventurous future that seemed just around the corner in the 1960s, through a more introspective period in the 1970s and the dystopian visions of the 1980s, all the way up to the more moderate and perhaps realistic visions that seem to pervade the 21st Century, of a future that is full of potential, but also requires hard work to achieve. Through every future past, *Doctor Who* has always ultimately affirmed that humanity will not just survive, but will prosper and conquer the stars.

DAVID JOHNSON

Gender, Science and Society

From the very beginning, *Doctor Who* has prominently featured companions alongside the Doctor, and overwhelmingly the majority of these have been female. This is not by any means to dismiss the male companions, from Ian Chesterton, Steven Taylor, Ben Jackson and Jamie McCrimmon in the 1960s through the ill-fated Adric in the early 1980s to Captain Jack Harkness and Mickey Smith in the early 2000s. But the male companions, with the possible exception of Captain Jack as played by the incomparable Jon Barrowman, fall into fairly standard male roles, such as the muscle to get out of a scrape, or the uncertain youth that blossoms under the tutelage of the Doctor. With the female companions, it is different; they have run a wide gamut. Admittedly, the 'screamer' who is perpetually in trouble has been a common motif; and perhaps because of this, *Doctor Who* has sometimes been accused of being sexist. While there is a possible case to be made there, it is not nearly as interesting as another perspective on the female companions. Because there have been so many, in a very wide range of roles, it is possible to see just how society has changed with regard to women, particularly in scientific or technological roles.

To be certain, there have been women in science for a very long time. As previously noted, the remarkable Lady Ada Lovelace was an adept mathematician who developed some core principles of programming for Charles Babbage's Difference Engine in the mid-19th Century. Marie Curie was instrumental in the discovery of radium, and led exciting new research into the nature of radiation, although at great personal cost. However, these women and others like them through the early 20th Century are noteworthy exceptions in fields dominated by men. Never mind that during the First World War, and again during the Second, thousands and thousands of women stepped up to perform jobs previously thought to be solely in the realm of men, such as munitions manufacturing and aircraft assembly. These machinations were temporary, and only in times of greatest need, and were stopped as soon as practical. By the time *Doctor Who* premiered in 1963, women were more confined in social expectations and roles than they had been at any time since the turn of the century.

The women of 1963 were effectively expected to be homemakers. That was it. If a woman worked, as was frequently necessary when she was single, it was a foregone conclusion that the job would last only until a husband arrived, after which time, she was supposed to leave the workplace and take up the noble duties and domestic science of running a household. Further, the jobs available to women were limited, both in scope and in advancement. Secretarial work was acceptable, as was working as a shop assistant, in addition to the traditional professions of nursing and teaching. There wasn't much else. Further, there was little room for advancement in any of these positions. It was simply assumed that a man would necessarily run the business and administrative side of any venture.

There were voices of protest, though. In the US, Betty Friedan wrote an aggressive and controversial book, *The Feminine Mystique,* which described at some length in its first chapter 'the problem with no name'. Friedan asserted that women everywhere were unhappy with their lot in life as housewives, and despite the view that they were domestic scientists who had to know such things as the right cleaner to get stains out of the washing, and the best way to make their own bread, they felt unfulfilled and unchallenged. The book became a rallying point for what would become known as second-wave feminism on both sides of the Atlantic. At the time of its 1963 publication, however, it was fresh and new, and no radical revolts had taken place just yet.

Into this environment step the first two female companions of *Doctor Who*: Susan Foreman and Barbara Wright, played by Carole Ann Ford and Jacqueline Hill respectively. While not expressly stated, events make it clear that Barbara is a single woman, working as a teacher at Coal Hill School. Despite this, she still displays a motherly instinct in her concern for Susan and her puzzling behaviour in class. However, Susan is the more interesting figure of the two. As the Doctor's granddaughter, she is the 'unearthly child' of the first episode's title, and has a curious mix of traits. She knows incredible amounts about certain parts of history, and almost nothing about others. She is also remarkably adept at science, expressing boredom when Ian instructs his pupils to test acidity with litmus paper, and frustration when he asks them to solve an equation in three dimensions – she asserts that the problem is unsolvable using only A, B, and C, but instead requires also D and E, representing time and space. The concerns that Ian and Barbara's have about Susan prompt them to investigate; and, of course, the rest is history, so to speak.

But Susan's character continues to be of interest during the first two seasons of *Doctor Who*, although not for the original reasons. It would appear, given her introduction, that she should be a remarkably capable young woman, who could face countless problems with, if not aplomb, at least a degree of competence. It is remarkable how quickly her persona degrades to being a shrill screamer in regular need of rescuing. Even in the remaining three episodes of the first serial, '100,000 BC', she has little to do other than grow frantic about missing her grandfather, run through the Stone Age forest and generally look worried. It is worth noting, though, that at the conclusion of '100,000 BC', it is Susan who discerns the means for the travellers to escape from danger, putting a skull on a flaming torch to create an eerie effect that scares the tribesmen holding them prisoner. In the next serial, commonly known as 'The Daleks', she also displays some bravery when she goes out into the dead forest of the planet Skaro to get anti-radiation drugs from the TARDIS and befriends the indigenous Thal people. By

'The Keys of Marinus', however, she is reduced to shrill whining; a fact not lost on Carole Ann Ford herself. She largely remains in such roles through to her departure in 'The Dalek Invasion of Earth'.

One might ask why this is so. If the whole premise of Ian's and Barbara's involvement with the Doctor is based on Susan's unearthly behaviour and knowledge, why then does she wind up being the first of many 'scream queens' in *Doctor Who*? The most likely answer is simply that the writers didn't know how to deal with her character as she was initially presented.[62] Admittedly, it is a difficult balance to find between a companion who is intelligent and capable and one who needs to be rescued, and this problem manifests itself repeatedly throughout both runs of *Doctor Who*. In Susan's case, it was easier to err on the side of rescue-needing than that of independent woman, even though the Doctor in 1963 is not quite the dashing adventurer he would become in later incarnations. Barbara, too, seems to need a lot of rescuing in the first two seasons, more often by Ian than by the Doctor, but perhaps this is forgivable, given her terrestrial origins. But Susan really should have been able to cope better than she did with Daleks, Voords and the French Revolution, given her mysterious but otherworldly origins.

Susan was also the first companion to leave the TARDIS, departing early in the second season. Her departure, in the second serial of that season, set the tone for the programme's future, where the producers would bring a steady stream of new companion characters in to travel with the Doctor, instead of relying on a fixed cast and crew. Carole Ann Ford left the programme because she felt her character was not developing much, a fact acknowledged in a memo from the BBC's Head of Drama, Sydney Newman, on 28 October 1964, in which he wished her luck and hoped to see her in the BBC again 'in roles

---

[62] Susan Kay. 'Why Can't They Write for Women?' *The Stage and Television Today*. (London) 19 November 1964, 11.

other than that of the "waif from outer space".'[63] More significantly, in the fiction of the programme, Susan left the TARDIS for reason that was much more stereotypical in the early 1960s – she left to get married. Granted, the human she left to marry was living in a desolate future Earth that had been devastated by Daleks, so the prospect of a humble and happy home was not immediately on the horizon for her, but it nevertheless reinforced the 1960s perception that once a woman got married, she was expected to stop working and settle into her domestic duties. This is in very sharp contrast to the situation in Series Six and Seven of the revived programme, where married couple Amy and Rory continue their gallivanting across the universe with the Doctor.

Susan's departure, as the programme's first, was marked by a sentimental moment in which the Doctor makes a little speech sending his granddaughter on her way. This particular scene resonated enough with viewers that it was repeated at the opening of the twentieth anniversary special 'The Five Doctors', and even depicted in the fiftieth anniversary docudrama *An Adventure in Time and Space*, where in addition to David Bradley's performance as William Hartnell recreating the moment, the final scene encompasses Hartnell's own version of it as well. For all the popularity of the scene, it is hard not to see it as a little bit patronising in light of the development of later social norms, with the Doctor telling Susan her future lies with presumed future husband David rather than in the TARDIS, and that with David she will have a chance to put down roots instead of wandering forever. For all the touching sentimentality of the moment, and the reasonable grandfatherly feelings of the Doctor, it is still hard not to see Susan as a bit of a pawn here, locked out of the TARDIS and essentially told to go

---

[63] Sydney Newman, memo to Carole Ann Ford, 28 October 1964 as found on 'Moments in Time – Goodbye Susan, Goodbye My Dear.' *Doctor Who News*, 26 December 2014, accessed 27 December 2014. http://www.doctorwhonews.net/2014/12/moments-in-time-goodbye-susan-goodbye.html

get married. Similarly, when Ian and Barbara also leave the TARDIS, near the end of the second season, they return to their own time together and it is implied, though not stated, that they will explore the romantic tension that has been apparent between them.

By the end of the second season, the pattern had been set whereby companions could come and go through the TARDIS without fundamentally changing the programme's nature. Typically through the first two Doctors' runs, there were both male and female companions. The male companions served the role of action hero to their different female counterparts, many of whom were effectively just screamers, there to be terrified at an appropriate moment and then dashingly rescued just in time, usually. By 1966, though, the writers and producers were aware that the programme needed to modernise, to reflect the rapidly changing times the 1960s embodied. Arguably the character Dodo Chaplet represented the first real effort at this, being a modern, working-class young woman, although her accent was toned down after her initial appearance. But Dodo didn't seem to resonate with viewers or writers, and so she was unceremoniously written out during the Season Three finale, 'The War Machines'. This same serial introduced the second attempt at the modern woman, Polly, played by Anneke Wills.

Polly represented an attempt at a seismic shift for the programme, and a manifestation of the second-wave feminism that was rippling through society on both sides of the Pond at the time. She worked as a secretary, dressed in trendy 1960s style, and frequented a club where she knew how to deal with rude and chauvinistic men. Stylistically, she was a sort of emissary for the fashions popularised in the mid-1960s by designers such as Mary Quant, whose efforts drove the success of the mini-skirt and other youth-focused styles.[64] Unfortunately, in some ways she got little better treatment than

---

[64] 'Biography of Mary Quant.'
Victoria and Albert Museum, 2015, accessed 9 June 2015. http://www.vam.ac.uk/content/articles/m/mary-quant/

her predecessors had, in terms of her role within the TARDIS crew. While she was certainly able to be feisty whenever male companion Ben got on her nerves too much, and was brave and intelligent, she still was given little to do on the technical side of things. A telling example of this is found in William Hartnell's final serial as the Doctor, 'The Tenth Planet'. As the men from the TARDIS and an Antarctic research station prepare to battle the Cyberman menace, Polly's grand contribution to the effort is to offer to make coffee. A few serials later, when the Cybermen appear again in 'The Moonbase', Polly is relegated to nursing duties rather than given any sort of frontline role, and at one point is again sent off to make coffee; although, perhaps as a nod to changing times, she does come up with the idea of creating a solvent mix, referred to as 'Cocktail Polly', to attack the Cybermen, even though she doesn't know exactly what is in the nail polish remover she suggests using. Effectively this is little different from Susan's inspiration of the skulls on torches, where a woman has an idea that the men are supposed to execute. Still, her portrayal overall suggests that, socially, women were demanding a greater degree of freedom and equality than before.

Curiously, Polly's successor in the TARDIS was very much a throwback companion, in some ways literally. While Polly was very much a product of the late 1960s, Victoria Waterfield, as played by Deborah Watling, was a child of the Victorian era. In the stories, Victoria quickly adapts to more contemporary fashions in her adventures with the Doctor, but she is also the classic screamer, frequently left with little to do other than get rescued. She does at times show great courage that echoes Victorian heroines such as Mina Harker née Murray in *Dracula*; but, at the core of it all, she is the sheltered young woman that both the Doctor and male companion Jamie look after with great care and tenderness, and her choice to leave the Doctor for the comforts of family in 'Fury From the Deep' is consistent with earlier feminine models. The contrasts between Polly and Victoria demonstrate the struggle that *Doctor Who* had in terms of its female parts for much of the 1960s.

GENDER, SCIENCE AND SOCIETY

That struggle is significantly demonstrated by the last female companion during Patrick Troughton's time in the TARDIS. On a space station in the 26th Century, the Doctor meets Zoe Heriot, played by Wendy Padbury. Zoe is clearly technically quite adept, and scientifically quite literate and capable. This is repeatedly made clear to audiences, such as when Zoe is literally able to set a computer smoking by posing it a logical puzzle while trying to gain access to a building during the serial 'The Invasion'. Her intelligence is further shown when she is initially able to get a higher score than the Doctor in a mental ability test run by the nefarious Krotons in 'The Krotons'. As noted in an earlier chapter, *Doctor Who* excels at showcasing the prospective positive future for human kind, and Zoe represents the future of woman fully liberated, scientifically and technically literate, and able to use her knowledge to achieve a desired goal. So why does she scream so much?

The paradox of Zoe in *Doctor Who* is that, while she is clearly capable, she is also in some ways daft. Her ability to scream at the slightest provocation is remarkable, and she is given plenty of opportunities to do so, such as during the unusual 'fill-in' first episode of 'The Mind Robber'. Here, the production schedule found itself one episode short, so a one-off instalment was cobbled together to bridge 'The Dominators' and 'The Mind Robber'. At the end of the episode, the TARDIS suddenly explodes, leaving Zoe clutching the central console, along with Jamie, while she screams her way out of the scene. Later in the same serial, she finds herself in the Land of Fiction, trapped in nothing more than a giant glass jar with a piece of paper covering the top of it. While it is possible to rationalise this, in that the Master of the Land of Fiction may have altered her senses – the scene plays on the familiar riddle, 'When is a door not a door? When it's ajar' – even once the trap is uncovered and she can see where she really is, she still needs the Doctor and Jamie to remove the paper cover and help her out of it. However just a short while later, she defeats a comic-book hero known as the Karkus in hand-to-hand combat – which is not a trivial feat, given how buff the Karkus is supposed to be, although the muscle suit he wears is at best laughable.

Ultimately, the mix of Zoe's at times contradictory traits can be seen as mirroring the conflicts going on in the world at large at the end of the 1960s. The traditionalists of the time still wished to have women that fit the demure, weaker-sex image that had persisted since the end of the Second World War, while the progressives pushed further and further into new career fields and social roles for women. Zoe was a manifestation of both these often-incompatible roles. As the liberated woman of the distant future, by which time it was reasonable to assume women would be masters of science and technology, she could excel, but she still needed to fit the norms of the 1960s, which suggested women needed male help to accomplish many tasks in life.

With the format adjustment that *Doctor Who* underwent moving into Season Seven in 1970, the issue of women in technology and science roles became more pressing. When the season begins, the Doctor is exiled on Earth – mostly for BBC budgetary reasons – and a new companion enters the picture in the form of highly qualified Dr Liz Shaw. This was unabashedly new territory for the programme. The stories made it clear from the first that the events were set on a roughly-contemporary Earth. This meant that the characters interacting with the Doctor on television could also potentially be interacting with the world outside viewers' living rooms. In that context, Liz was perhaps a bit threatening. She was, obviously, a doctor, and a well-trained and disciplined scientist. She was also strong-willed, a fact not lost on Brigadier Lethbridge-Stewart from his first meeting with her at the beginning of her introductory story, 'Spearhead from Space'. As the Doctor and Liz settle down to figure out how to combat the Auton threat in that serial, it is clear that the Time Lord regards her as something much closer to a peer than any figure yet seen in the programme. However, it quickly becomes evident to Liz just how much more the Doctor knows about science than she does. This can be attributed to the time travel theme of the stories more than to any specific gender issue. Liz remains in the programme only until the end of Season Seven, though, and is not even given a proper send-off, with merely a passing reference to mark her absence at the start of Series Eight. From a social history context, it is fair to suggest that the rapid departure of Liz Shaw is a demonstration of just what the world was ready for, and not ready for, at that time. It is also perhaps fair to suggest that the programme's writers may not have known what to do with a strong-willed and technically literate woman who was unwilling simply to scream for help when danger appeared. Liz's replacement solved that writing problem quite handily.

Jo Grant was a remarkably popular companion, due in no small part to the talents of actress Katy Manning. She was also the antithesis of Liz Shaw – if not a vacuous bubble-head, she was at least not terribly bright much of the time, and much more inclined to need the usual rescuing. As the Brigadier notes in 'Terror of the Autons', what the Doctor really needs is not a peer, but someone to 'pass you your test tubes and tell you how brilliant you are'. Jo certainly fit the bill for the three series she was with the Doctor, before she left to get married, much as Susan had before. To be fair to Jo's character and to the writers of 1973, she at least went off to marry a scientist and go on an expedition seeking alternative food sources up the Amazon, instead of simply settling in to a routine of dusting, baking and child-raising.

For much of the rest of the 1970s, *Doctor Who* seemed to struggle with just what women were expected to be and do, much as society as a whole was struggling. Sarah Jane Smith, Jo's successor in the TARDIS and one of the most popular and enduring companions of both the classic programme and the revived version, was supposed to be an assertive and independent reporter, but wound up being little more than a variant on Jo and countless other companions in need of rescue. She routinely got trapped by some technological device, such as a sleeper bed in 'The Ark in Space' or a booby-trapped plastic tube in 'Pyramids of Mars'. Despite that, or perhaps because of it, she was the go-to figure for two spin-off programmes, and featured prominently in two stories of the revived programme. Within the second spin-off, *The Sarah Jane Adventures*, Jo Grant also made an appearance in the story 'The Death of the Doctor', although tellingly both ladies still needed the Doctor himself to come save them one last time. While Elisabeth Sladen's performance as Sarah Jane was commendable, and she created a genuine sense of empathy on screen, there was no real new ground broken during her stay in the TARDIS. Whether or not it was intentional, after Sarah Jane's exit in 'The Hand of Fear', the next two companions to travel with the Doctor came from very different extremes on the social spectrum of women.

The companions Leela and Romanadvoratrelunda, usually called Romana, represent the definition of diametrically opposed figures, and putting them into the overall context of the feminist issues of the 1970s makes them even more interesting. Leela comes aboard the TARDIS shortly after Sarah Jane's departure, helping the Doctor face off against a schizophrenic computer he inadvertently created during an earlier visit to her planet, as noted above. Leela, though, is part of the Sevateem, a group descended from the first survey team on the alien world, who have been forced to fall back on more savage instinct to survive in the harsh environment. She spends much of her subsequent time in the TARDIS clad in a leather bathing suit that leaves little to the imagination, and yet for all the 'cheesecake' of her attire, her main solution to a problem is to kill it. While it would be overzealous to attribute all of Leela's presentation to the aggressive feminism of the 1970s, it is also hard not to see her in that light. Much of the feminist movement was calling simply for equality and freedom for women, but there was a certain radical element on the fringes that advocated not just the supremacy of women but also in some cases the destruction of men. Valerie Solanis's *SCUM Manifesto*, from her Society for Cutting Up Men, most definitely falls into this latter category, as among the many weaknesses of men enumerated, she argues that they are 'not even suited for stud service.'[65] Leela's fierce demeanour, then, can

---

[65] Valerie Solanis. 'The SCUM Manifesto.' *Womynkind.org* accessed 29 April 2014. http://www.womynkind.org/scum.htm

be seen as a presentation of this hostile woman, willing to cut up men with her knife for her own ends, and not feel the least bit of remorse for doing it.

For all her fierce intensity, though, Leela is assuredly a fish out of water when it comes to the technological side of her adventures in *Doctor Who*. She seldom understands the technology she encounters, and simply takes it on faith that what the Doctor says is right. The Doctor, for his part, is almost patronising to Leela at times, such as in an early episode where he offers her a yo-yo because it might amuse her like some child. Unaware of what the yo-yo is, she feels she has to keep the motion going in order to keep the TARDIS in flight. Leela doesn't bat an eye at encountering Rutans, sentient space viruses or Sontarans, but neither does she ever seem to understand the exact nature of these enemies, and reacts by threatening them with violence.

Within the context of the aggressive woman, then, there is at least some degree of commentary that, no matter how fierce or independent the woman is, she will remain an ignorant savage, while the men of the world sort out the science and technology. This image is troublingly reinforced with Leela's departure at the end of 'The Invasion of Time', when she helps the Doctor fend off a Sontaran invasion of Gallifrey, then opts to stay behind because she has fallen in love with a Time Lord named Andred. This resolution to her character arc is not only laughably implausible, but also harks right back to the departure of Susan in 'The Dalek Invasion of Earth'. Leela is not even given the opportunity for further adventures, as Jo Grant was, but instead is somehow expected to settle into domestic bliss in what is perhaps the most staid and boring civilisation in the universe outside of Karn, surrounded by technology that her adventures with the Doctor suggest she will never understand properly.

Next to join the TARDIS was a character who was nearly the exact opposite of Leela. This was Romana, admirably played by Mary Tamm. Romana was the first attempt since Liz Shaw to give the Doctor a peer as a companion. She is a Time Lady, albeit a much younger one than the Doctor at only about 125 years old. Despite her relative youth, she is clearly not just comfortable with technology, but able to master it. She uses a device given to her by the nearly omnipotent White Guardian to locate segments of the Key to Time, flies the TARDIS when needed, and is readily able to cope with androids, space pirates and even the threat of a planetary armageddon. This first version of Romana is a remarkably independent but also approachable woman, in contrast to the fiercely aggressive and potentially radically feminist Leela. Instead of being from the feminist fringe, she is a depiction of the moderate feminist, willing and able to embark on adventures on her own, comfortable standing her ground against the men she encounters, and generally attempting to take the world on her own terms.

Unfortunately, the world, or at least the programme's writers, didn't seem quite ready for this, and Romana wound up being written into passivity more than once. Gender roles are set in the first few moments of her opening serial, 'The Ribos Operation', as she protests about the Doctor calling her Romana, and says she would prefer 'Fred' to that. The Doctor says, 'Fine. Come on, Romana,' setting the tone for much of what is to follow. More poignant are the situations in which Romana finds herself as she and the Doctor search for the Key to Time across the full set of serials in Season Sixteen. While she is quite comfortable in the TARDIS, and boasts about her grades from the Academy on Gallifrey, she can't seem to cope with run-of-the-mill events when she is outside the ship. In 'The Ribos Operation', a simple mechanical door partly closes, trapping her in a room with a fierce beast known as a Shrivenzale, and for some reason Romana is unable to figure out that she can crawl under the door, instead waiting for the Doctor to rescue her. Later, in 'The Stones of Blood', she opts to go jaunting about in some very stylish but markedly impractical high heels, and promptly falls over the edge of a cliff for no apparent reason. In 'The Androids of Tara', she sets off on her own to recover the latest segment of the Key to Time, and is quickly captured by a nefarious local prince, after which she spends a great deal of time in a prison cell with her doppelganger, peacefully learning how to weave instead of trying to escape. Rather than all this being considered an indictment of Romana's character, it is perhaps more suitably seen as a manifestation of the conflicting pressures *Doctor Who* was facing in light of the changing world in the later 1970s.

By that time, a strong and intelligent woman in a media role was seen as not only acceptable but even desirable, in part because strong and intelligent women were socially acceptable as well. It is a mistake to think that suddenly in 1977 all women were empowered, liberated bastions of feminine might. As in any time period, and for any part of society, the women of the 1970s fell into a spectrum from the ultra conservative, who favoured traditional gender roles and dress, to the extremely progressive, who promoted a sort of androgyny and a gender-free society. But the norm of society had demonstrably shifted by the later 1970s, so that it was not especially difficult to find a woman as a physician, or as a professor of calculus, and the media presentation of society needed to shift to accommodate that new norm. It is hardly a coincidence that the only live-action portrayal of American superhero Wonder Woman prior to 2016 ran during the same time period.

The problem was how to fit this intelligent and strong woman into the formula of *Doctor Who*. Part of the success of characters like Sarah Jane and Jo was that they were empathetic but still plausibly in need of rescuing when the aliens threatened. Leela was much less plausible in the latter regard, although her unfamiliarity with technology could be used to create situations where she could not stab her way out of trouble. Romana, though, posed the same sort of challenge for *Doctor Who* as Liz Shaw had in 1970. The programme still hadn't quite got the knack of fitting the modern woman Romana was supposed to be into an established formula that required having a damsel in distress. *Doctor Who* was going to need to modernise, somehow, to keep plausible female characters in the mix.

The first attempt to cope with this challenge was to get a new Romana. Mary Tamm left after one series, as her goal of creating a character different from the previous companions had largely fallen flat, but the production team still liked the idea of a Time Lady companion. The obvious solution was to allow Romana to regenerate – although, as with Liz Shaw, there was no formal send-off for Mary Tamm's Romana. Instead, the opening of Season Seventeen simply introduced a regenerated Romana, appearing in the form of the character Princess Astra from the last Season Sixteen story, 'The Armageddon Factor' – obliquely demonstrating in the process that Romana was more technically savvy than the Doctor, by being able to control her regeneration more precisely than he ever could. Thus actress Lalla Ward, who had played Princess Astra, now stepped into the TARDIS as a new version of Romana, still technically and scientifically literate, but with a much more demure personality that better fitted the model *Doctor Who* needed, wherein the Doctor could still save the companion and save the day. Despite some story highlights from Romana II's first season, most notably in the popular serial 'City of Death', *Doctor Who* was soon facing declining viewing numbers, and it was clear change had to come, and in more than just the way gender roles were presented.

That change came with new producer John Nathan-Turner and Season Eighteen. Nathan-Turner set about bringing *Doctor Who* into the 1980s, and with him came a very different dynamic in the TARDIS. Over the course of this season, Romana left the TARDIS to embark on a series of adventures of her own, and new companions Adric, Nyssa and Tegan came on board. This new set of regulars left the TARDIS with a larger crew than it had had since William Hartnell was at the console as the first Doctor, and presented a fresh approach to the way companions interacted with the science and technology of the stories, as well as with each other.

Adric, as played by Matthew Waterhouse, was the first of the new companions to come aboard, and the first male companion in the TARDIS since Harry Sullivan in 1975. He wore a badge for mathematical excellence, which would seem to support the notion of male superiority in maths and sciences, but he was also a very young traveller, and seems to have stepped into the role of the female 'screamers' of the 1960s. In a way, Adric served the same purpose as Susan did in 1963, as the remarkably bright teenager who could also create plot complications when necessary, due to his inexperience and tendency to whinge on about things. The change in gender marked a notable shift for the programme, as Adric would have a significant counterpoint in the next new companion to step into the TARDIS.

Nyssa, played by Sarah Sutton, was initially intended to be a one-off character for the serial 'The Keeper of Traken', which served primarily to bring back the Master as a recurring *Doctor Who* villain. But Nathan-Turner decided she should have a continuing role in the TARDIS, so she was brought back in the next serial, Tom Baker's swansong 'Logopolis', and remained with Peter Davison's version of the Doctor through the middle of Season Twenty. Nyssa is young, like Adric, and technically literate; she shows an interest in bio-engineering, and is bright enough to have developed a molecular adjustment tool that the Doctor admires and promptly pockets. Unlike Adric, however, she is a quiet, studious, dependable type, and far less likely than past companions to wind up screaming for help.

Tegan, played by Janet Fielding, was the last of the new companion set to join up, and then only reluctantly from her character's point of view. In one sense, Tegan is the most like previous female companions, in that she too is not terribly knowledgeable from a scientific or technological standpoint, and is the most likely to scream for the Doctor when the aliens appear; but there are also some noteworthy differences. In particular, Tegan is a strongly career-orientated woman, albeit that her career as a flight stewardess is not at first glance a terribly liberated one. She is also fiercely assertive in her dealings with the Doctor and others.

This trio of companions would serve only one series together in the TARDIS, but demonstrated a noticeable gender shift in the way they interacted with each other and with technology. The gender reversal is obvious from the start, as Adric's mathematical ability is exploited by the Master in the post-regeneration story 'Castrovalva', while Nyssa is the one to save the Doctor by using her molecular bonding tool to craft a 'zero cabinet' that allows his dendrites to heal in an environment free from interference. Two serials later, in 'Kinda', Adric continues his awkwardness with technology by running amok with a survival suit that has the potential to kill people. Nyssa serves as a counterpoint to Adric in 'The Visitation', when the Doctor tasks her with developing the technological solution to combat a powerful android in 17th Century England. Nyssa dutifully retires to the TARDIS, constructs an appropriate sonic device, and successfully blasts the android to bits without any male help. In Nyssa's final story, 'Terminus', part-way through the following season, she contracts a deadly plague that allows the programme-makers to indulge in a rare 'cheesecake' moment for her character, as her fever compels her to strip down to a skimpy bit of lingerie by the end of the story. More significantly, though, she leaves the Doctor not for love or to settle down, but because her skills and abilities are best suited to help the other people with the plague. Adric, on the other hand, has already died a relatively pointless death in the story 'Earthshock', trying to use his mathematical skills to save a crashing space freighter, unaware that the crash is actually necessary for human history to unfold as it should.

This gender reversal that Adric and Nyssa demonstrate on board the TARDIS during the early 1980s is partially offset by Tegan. She continues to serve admirably as the best effort yet at a modern damsel in distress, most notably in her interactions with the malevolent Mara in 'Kinda' and the later 'Snakedance'. However, little else changes for her role, even with the addition of a new companion in the person of Vislor Turlough, played by Mark Strickson. Turlough, like Adric, is a technically adept young man from an alien world, and like Adric he tends to be a bit of a whiner at times. For much of Season Twenty and into Season Twenty-One, Turlough and Tegan largely follow the established model of being intelligent but regularly in need of rescuing. But with their departure near the end of Peter Davison's time in the TARDIS, change came yet again.

The new companion, Perpugilliam Brown, or Peri for short, was a step backward in terms of gender roles and technical ability compared even with Tegan's modest presentation in those areas. Played by Nicola Bryant, she featured the whiny aspects of Adric and Turlough, the limited intelligence of Jo Grant but without the empathy, and a dubious American accent, all rolled into a companion of uncertain value to the fifth Doctor, although she seemed to make for a better foil to the sixth. However, at this time, a new figure was brought into the programme who was much more interesting than Peri and demonstrated some of the underlying gender-role changes of the 1980s. This was the female Time Lord known as the Rani. While superficially she appeared to be just a kind of female version of the Master, the comparison breaks down on closer inspection.

The Rani, superbly played by Kate O'Mara, debuted opposite Anthony Ainely's incarnation of the Master in the serial 'The Mark of the Rani'. Like the Master, she is a renegade; but she has very different aspirations. She already rules her own planet at the start of the story, and is visiting Industrial Revolution-era England only in order to harvest from human brains some chemicals she requires to overcome a problem controlling her subjects. Her purpose is very focused, and she sees the Doctor more as a nuisance to her plans than as a significant antagonist. She has even less flattering views on the Master, considering him a bumbler with an irrational desire to exact revenge upon the Doctor at all costs. Although she agrees to an alliance with the Master at one point, this is only because he has stolen away from her the vial of chemicals she has spent so much time collecting from the humans. As the action progresses, she increasingly emasculates him, in the end reducing him to a sort of stooge-like caricature. Despite her clever mind and focused objective, and perhaps because of the Master's intervention in her plans, the Doctor is able to get one step ahead of the duo and send the Rani's TARDIS hurtling to the far reaches of the universe – although she would return in Season Twenty-Four to confront a newly regenerated Doctor, played by Sylvester McCoy.

The Rani definitely set a new tone for the way women were portrayed in *Doctor Who*. Certainly she had to be defeated each time she appeared, but within that limit she represented an opposing peer to the Doctor. She was equipped with comparable technology and comparable technological prowess, and was an effective equal in intellectual terms. In short, she was everything Peri was not, and because she was not a companion to the Doctor, she was unfettered by any need to be rescued, although she also could never win. Despite the limits her malevolent nature imposed, the Rani was popular enough to be the villain of choice for the brief thirtieth anniversary *Doctor Who* skit 'Dimensions in Time', broadcast as part of the *Children in Need* telethon for 1993.

With the final companion shown in the classic programme, the writers and producer finally found the right balance for the late 1980s. Actress Sophie Aldred's presentation of the boisterous young woman nicknamed Ace had the right mix of intelligence, independence and a touch of naivety to work perfectly as a modernised woman for *Doctor Who*. Ace can be seen as a curious composite of some of the features of previous companions, following in the footsteps of Susan, Polly, Liz, Leela, Romana and Tegan. She has her own mysterious past, one the Doctor had a hand in, as revealed in 'The Curse of Fenric', which invites a degree of comparison to Susan, though without the distinct familial connection. She has a fierce sense of independence and a tendency to blow things up, which suggest a comparison to Leela. However, Ace is by no means technophobic or even technically impaired, as she is quite comfortable around computers and outlandish gadgets, as Liz and Romana both were. She dresses in very modern, tomboyish attire, drawing from her own fashion plate as Polly did, and is unabashedly assertive like Tegan, but manages not to come across as rude most of the time. Into the mix, Ace adds her own brand of recklessness, and is able and willing to lead the charge when needed, yet still presents as a figure who plausibly needs rescuing from time to time by 'the Professor', as she calls the Doctor. All the elements fused, if not perfectly, at least remarkably well.

While classic *Doctor Who* drew to a close at the end of Season Twenty-Six, with Ace and the Doctor heading off into the sunset, the tone Ace set for companions served as a demonstration of how far the programme and society as whole had come since 1963. By 1989, women were not only allowed to be but were expected to be technically literate to at least some degree, independent without being arrogant, and capable of standing up against the malevolent forces of the universe, albeit still with some degree of guidance from the Doctor. The final tone of the classic programme, in terms of companions, would also serve as a model both for the 1996 TV movie and for the later revival in 2005. In the case of the former, the companion Grace Holloway, played by Daphne Ashbrook, is a medical doctor in a large hospital, confident enough in her position to stand up to dodgy administrators; and once convinced of the dire nature of the situation with the regenerated Doctor, she wholeheartedly embarks on efforts to help him save the world. With only a single screen appearance, Grace being unwilling to board the TARDIS at the end of the movie, she might well have been just another one-off stronger female character. However, she was just a precursor to what was to come with the revival.

With the restart of *Doctor Who* in 2005, it was clear from the very first that the screamer companions were long gone. Rose Tyler certainly could blunder into trouble, as she does in a basement full of Autons in her introductory episode, 'Rose', but she could also adapt quickly, and dish out as good as she got, swinging from a chain to save the Doctor during his confrontation with the Nestene Consciousness. She is intelligent enough to hold her own in a deadly game show in the 'The Long Game'. She is empowered enough to act boldly, too, as in the first series finale, 'The Parting of the Ways', where she, not the Doctor, ultimately destroys the new Daleks, directing energy absorbed from the TARDIS against their fleet and disintegrating it. Further, Rose is adept with a mobile phone as well as a computer, and understands some basic scientific principles, as would be expected of anyone in the 21st Century, regardless of gender. She is not the least bit fazed when the Doctor is able to slip a gadget into her phone that allows her to call her mum up from a space station five billion years in the future.

Perhaps the most important demonstration of Rose as an empowered 21st Century woman is found in 'Rose' itself. She is already in somewhat of a stable relationship with her boyfriend Mickey, but opts to leave him to travel with the Doctor. This is the exact opposite of what happened with previous companions Susan, Jo and Leela. In fact, Rose even has the opportunity to confront those kinds of stereotypes directly in the Series Two story 'The Idiot's Lantern'. When she and the Doctor come to a London household to try to watch the coronation of Queen Elizabeth II on television, then a new invention, she minces no words confronting the boorish and prejudiced man of the house, ultimately empowering the put-upon wife to stand up for herself in ways decidedly out of character for the 1950s, but well within the gender norms of the early 21st Century.

While all of the companions in the revived programme are feisty in their own ways, and are technically literate as well as markedly independent, there is one figure that stands out as the capstone of the change both *Doctor Who* and society as a whole have undergone with regard to women in a technological context. While Martha Jones is noble, tough and clever, Donna Noble is feisty, aggressive and confident, Amy Pond is proud, witty and independent and Clara Oswald is coy, determined and technologically brilliant, River Song stands above them all as the ultimate manifestation of a woman with the right stuff. Admirably played by Alex Kingston, River is the first person to be presented as a full peer of the Doctor and actually pull off the role. The world was simply not quite ready for Liz Shaw, and Romana I was quickly and unfortunately pressed into the stereotypical companion role rather than allowed to fulfil the promise her character had. The Rani certainly managed to emasculate the Master, but never really quite convinced viewers she was a true equal to the Doctor, because in the end she had to lose the battle with him. With River, though, viewers are never quite certain who is gaming whom through her entire storyline.

The very creative premise for this storyline – that, as mentioned earlier, they are coming at each other from opposite ends of their timestreams – occasionally gives River the striking opportunity to know more than the Doctor does. Further, while River spends a large part of her time in prison (for the crime of killing the Doctor, although his death was actually just faked), she views this as merely an inconvenience and demonstrates repeatedly that she can leave her cell at will, even going so far as to comment that she is 'breaking in, not out' at one point in 'A Good Man Goes to War'. River can also fly the TARDIS better than the Doctor, and even do things with it that the Doctor has said are impossible, such as getting a monitoring circuit to work through a cloaking shield in 'The Impossible Astronaut'.

Effectively, River Song is the embodiment of the modern, fully capable woman that is common enough in the 21st Century to be not even remarked upon anymore. Women work not only as physicians, professors and technicians but also as chemists, field biologists, computer programmers, mathematicians, palaeontologists, geneticists and a host of other professions than even 25 years ago might have seemed far-fetched as careers for them. This is not to say western civilisation is completely gender-normed. Repeated studies have shown that women generally earn less than men, and many of the technical fields are still gender-skewed toward men. But women are there, doing chemical analyses on oil fields, designing computer chips, teaching advanced calculus and digging up rare dinosaur fossils. It would be difficult to attribute any of this progressive change for women to portrayals in *Doctor Who*. Instead, what *Doctor Who* provides is a long mirror by which women of the 21st Century can look back at what the social norms were more than fifty years ago, and observe just how much the world and social expectations have changed, allowing them opportunities today that even the unearthly child Susan Foreman might have been hard-pressed to imagine, given her perspective in 1963.

DAVID JOHNSON

Media and *Doctor Who*

Doctor Who is, obviously, a television programme; or rather, the heart of what *Doctor Who* has become in 2015 is a television programme. As it moves forward into its second fifty years, clearly it is not *just* a television programme, but an entire media empire that includes television, audio adventures, novelisations, comic books, computer games, internet websites, toys, collectible memorabilia, fan-written fiction publications, dedicated conventions and the theme-park-styled *Doctor Who Experience* in Cardiff. Few creations in the world have such a broad media reach as *Doctor Who* has in 2015. That was certainly not always so, however, and its evolution serves as a way to evaluate the increasing scale of mass media over the past fifty years.

When the programme went through its initial development and production run, there was no indication that it would become the media sensation of later years. In fact, there was more than one occasion when *Doctor Who* almost passed into history without much more than a footnote in a BBC production log. It is well documented that its principal creator, BBC Head of Drama Sydney Newman, took a risk in placing a woman, Verity Lambert, as its original producer. This immediately set it up for closer scrutiny within the BBC than it might otherwise have had to endure. Further, early pre-production issues and squabbles over budgeting could have scuttled the programme before any episode had aired, or even after the successful completion and broadcast of the first few serials.

For all *Doctor Who*'s early production limitations, including small studio space, relatively primitive editing facilities and modest funding per episode, in some ways it was a very forward-looking programme. The opening title sequence, based on a video-feedback effect that involved a camera being pointed at its own monitor while contrast and brightness controls were manipulated and lighting or other effects were introduced to the frame, was unlike any seen before it on the BBC. The first episode, 'An Unearthly Child', suggested that this was supposed to represent what the travellers inside the TARDIS experienced when it moved through space and time, although no mention of this was made again. The effect was well received in critical reviews of 'An Unearthly Child', although generally the rest of the episode was given only middling feedback with an admission that the programme had potential.[66]

The production process on the first several seasons of *Doctor Who* was very different from what it would become, both later in the classic programme and most definitely in the revived programme. The schedule was gruelling, and potentially debilitating, as William Hartnell would find out. 'An Unearthly Child' debuted on 23 November 1963, and the final Season One episode was broadcast on 12 September 1964. Then, after a scant break, Season Two premiered on 31 October 1964. This nearly year-round production schedule would be difficult enough to maintain, producing one episode per week, even with 21st Century studio equipment, but the BBC of 1963, while thoroughly modern in the sense of the 1960s, had no such luxuries. Each episode was rehearsed during the early part of a week, and the actual recording took place on the Friday evening of that week, done mostly as-live. The episode was videotaped, to be certain, but the technology was expensive and primitive, and any edits to the tape had to be made physically, with cut and splice, rather than through any electronic means. Any particularly complex scene would have to be captured previously on film, and then the film played in at the appropriate moment in the episode during the taping run on the Friday evening. Given

---

[66] Marjorie Norris. 'Meant for children but this will get a much wider audience.' *The Stage and Television Today*. (London) 5 December 1963, as found on http://cuttingsarchive.org/images/a/a5/1963-12-05_Stage_and_Television_Today.jpg

all this, it's amazing the programme came out looking as good as it did.

And how was this programme being received in 1963? Televisions were common household items in the UK by that time, although not quite yet ubiquitous. By 1963, there were approximately 16.7 million black-and-white television sets in the country.[67] Colour would not come to the BBC until 1966.[68] The picture tube was small, averaging 25 centimetres or so across the diagonal of the screen, but this may have been a bit of an advantage at the time, as the BBC broadcast its programmes at only 405 lines of resolution, the original standard for the UK – substantially lower than the 625 lines of the PAL standard that would be introduced in the late 1960s and come to fill the British airwaves until the advent of HD broadcasting in the early 21st Century. The 405-line resolution is also noticeably lower than the 525-line American NTSC broadcast standard of the time period. Consequently the smaller television screen size did not present a significant problem. If the screen had been scaled up much in size, the images on it would have appeared indistinct, as they do today when episodes from the first few seasons of *Doctor Who* are viewed on a large television – although the fact that the episodes now exist only as film transfers made for overseas sale purposes, rather than as original videotape masters, is also a factor in that.

Given the scale and cost of videotape technology in the high-end television studios of the BBC, it is patently clear that no-one in the viewing audience would have been making home video recordings of *Doctor Who* in 1963, or even in 1973. This is not to say that people did not make an effort to preserve favourite stories. Reel-to-reel audio tape recorders were becoming more commonplace in the 1960s, and some people who had these

---

[67] 'Television ownership in private domestic households 1956-2014 (millions)' *Broadcast Audience Research Board*, accessed 23 April 2015. http://www.barb.co.uk/resources/tv-facts/tv-ownership

[68] '1966: BBC tunes in to colour.' *BBC News*, 2008, accessed 23 April 2015.

http://news.bbc.co.uk/onthisday/hi/dates/stories/march/3/newsid_2514000/2514719.stm

devices used them to capture the soundtracks of *Doctor Who* episodes. In some cases, these audio recordings are all that remain of early episodes, after the videotapes at the BBC were recycled and the film copies destroyed. The process of recording television audio successfully off air using reel-to-reel tape is at best cumbersome, so the fact that some members of the audience were willing to try this is suggestive of the potential *Doctor Who* had to grow into different media.

Certainly, the Daleks helped spread the reach of the programme. While the first serial set in the Stone Age was a moderate success, the second secured *Doctor Who*'s place in the BBC line-up for quite some time. In the programme's early years, each individual episode carried its own title, but collectively the seven-part serial became known as 'The Daleks', and the reaction in the UK was wholly astonishing. The now-iconic enemies took hold of the public imagination in a way that few things ever had, creating a phenomenon referred to as Dalekmania, mirroring the Beatlemania that was sweeping both the UK and the US. In short order after the story's success, a plethora of Dalek toys came available in the shops, as well as a Dalek playsuit, and a novelisation of the serial.[69] The latter was significantly different from any other *Doctor Who* novelisation that followed it, inasmuch as it was designed as a stand-alone book, and so offers a completely different origin story from the previously-aired serial '100,000 BC', and is told from Ian's point of view.[70] Several ideas are presented in the narrative that never made it into the television programme, such as the Doctor having invented perpetual matches and a small personal grooming machine that moves across the user's hair, keeping it trimmed. Presumably these differences were allowed as there was no expectation that *Doctor Who* tie-in books would have a long future. Events proved otherwise, as two further novelisations – *Doctor Who and the Zarbi*

---

[69] 'Dalek Toy History.' *doctorwhotoys.net* accessed 23 July 2014. http://www.doctorwhotoys.net/dalektoyhistory.htm
[70] David Whitaker. *Doctor Who and the Daleks*. (UK: BBC Books/Random House, 1964, 2011), 1-16.

and *Doctor Who and the Crusaders* – followed in 1965; a highly successful series of novelisations from Target Books was launched in the 1970s; and ranges of original novels were added later on.

In addition to novels and toys, the mid-1960s fascination with the Daleks led to the licensing of two *Doctor Who* cinema films, *Dr Who and the Daleks* and *Daleks – Invasion Earth: 2150 AD*, the scripts of which adapted the first two Dalek television serials. In these, the main character is named and addressed as Doctor Who, rather than the Doctor, and a further revision to the origins of the main characters is offered. Doctor Who is a human who has invented 'TARDIS', not 'the TARDIS', and Barbara and Susan are both his granddaughters. In the first film, Ian is a nearly hopeless bumbler courting Barbara, and both of them are much younger than they were portrayed in the television programme. Susan is younger still, around the age of ten. The films can perhaps be best seen as attempts at cashing in on the Daleks' popularity. Despite this, Peter Cushing's portrayal of Doctor Who has continued to occupy at least a niche-space in the *Doctor Who* universe to the present day. Both films are still available in Blu-ray and digital download formats, and in 2014 a fan-fiction annual of stories for Doctor Who came out. Within the programme's fandom, there are even occasional debates about how the two films might be incorporated into the main *Doctor Who* canon (to the extent that such a thing actually exists).

As a preview of the global phenomenon that *Doctor Who* would become in the 21st Century, the 1960s saw the programme move into about as wide a range of media as possible. The television programme, the novelisations, official BBC annuals, weekly comic-strip adventures in *TV Comic*, the films, a stage production called *The Curse of the Daleks* in the 1965-1966 holiday season, as well as all the associated merchandising, really did represent nearly the full spectrum of media opportunities available at the time.[71] The only place *Doctor Who* had no significant presence was on BBC radio, although recently-discovered materials show that a series was discussed in 1967.[72] As there were as yet no ready means of having home copies of television programmes, the media penetration of *Doctor Who* was quite thorough – in the UK.

That geographical limitation was a key factor. The BBC did distribute film copies of the early *Doctor Who* serials to many nations worldwide, primarily in the British Commonwealth, with broadcasts taking place in Australia, New Zealand and Canada among others. This has been a resoundingly good thing from the point of view of archivists looking to recover episodes lost during the later purges of the BBC archives. But *Doctor Who* stayed largely a British attraction into the 1970s. With the coming of the colour era and Jon Pertwee, there was an abortive attempt to distribute the programme in the US, but this met with only limited success. No further efforts were made to get *Doctor Who* to the US until Tom Baker's tenure in the TARDIS.

Tom Baker's arrival marked a turning point for *Doctor Who*, although not right away. From a strictly technical point of view, little changed with the handover from Pertwee to Baker. The production scheduled had changed from 40-plus episodes per year to a more modest 25-plus episodes per year at the same time the programme had moved into colour, and the same budgetary limitations that had left the Doctor largely stranded on Earth for several seasons were still in place when the fourth Doctor bounded onto the screen with episode one of 'Robot' at the end of 1974. But there was something about the wild-eyed enthusiasm

---

[71] Harold Jackson. '*The Curse of the Daleks* at Wyndham's.' *Guardian*. 22 December 1965, page unknown, as found at *Cuttings Archive*, accessed 1 May 2015.
http://cuttingsarchive.org/index.php/The_Curse_of_the_Daleks_at_Wyndham%27s

[72] Chuck Foster. 'Missing Radio Script Discovered.' *Doctor Who News*, 15 January 2012, accessed 23 April 2015.
http://www.doctorwhonews.net/2012/01/dwn150112121012-missing-radio-script.html

Tom Baker brought to the role that energised the entire media universe of *Doctor Who*.

The Target Books novelisation line, which had been launched in 1974, saw amazing success during Tom Baker's time in the TARDIS in the later 1970s.[73] Marvel Comics in the UK explored a new media outlet with a periodical, initially known as *Doctor Who Weekly*, in 1979, featuring articles, photos and new comic-strip adventures with Tom Baker's incarnation of the Doctor.[74] The periodical shifted to monthly format in 1980, and has continued publication to the present day, although the nature of the content has evolved as the programme has. Also during the Tom Baker years, the *Doctor Who* Appreciation Society (DWAS) was formed in 1976; and again it continues to the present day, currently with Colin Baker as the honorary president.[75] And, as mentioned, Tom Baker's stories also served as the vehicle for *Doctor Who* to make its first successful foray into the US.

In 1978, the first four seasons of Tom Baker's run in *Doctor Who* were being distributed in the US to affiliates of the Public Broadcasting System, commonly referred to as PBS.[76] It is worth noting that PBS itself never sent the programme out, nor mandated its broadcast by individual stations operating within its network. This meant that the programme's US distribution was spotty at best in the late 1970s and much of the early 1980s; but in those markets where it aired, it attracted what can be

---

[73] 'Target Books.' *TARDIS Data Core*, accessed 9 August 2014. http://tardis.wikia.com/wiki/Target_Books

[74] '*Doctor Who Magazine* wins Guinness World Record.' *Doctor Who News*, 1 October 2010, accessed 9 August 2014. http://www.doctorwhonews.net/2010/04/doctor-who-magazine-wins-guinness-world.html

[75] 'Celestial Archive.' *Doctor Who* Appreciation Society, accessed 9 August 2014. http://www.dwasonline.co.uk/celestial_archive

[76] Jenkins, Alan. 'For 14 years now, a science fiction program, *Doctor Who* has been frightening and entertaining children in Britain.' *The Palm Beach Post* (Palm Beach, FL), 26 August 1978, TV1-2. PDF.

considered a cult following.[77] A change in distribution format for the serials may have contributed to this, as well. In the US, the programme could be run in its original 25-minute episode format, but it was also offered in an omnibus or feature-length format, where an entire four-part serial was edited together into one 90-minute product. While purists might argue that the omnibus format robs *Doctor Who* of its signature cliffhangers, it allowed viewers to see a whole story in a single sitting, which appealed to some in the US. Regardless of the format of presentation, Tom Baker's Doctor was enough of a hit in the US to prompt PBS stations to secure earlier stories from the 1960s and 1970s, as well as to get new seasons when they became available.

It is difficult to place the US success of *Doctor Who* in a proper context, but it is fair to suggest that it did much for the programme's long-term survival. This is not to make the US out to be some great media bastion, or to suggest that something is not successful until it is successful in the US. Indeed, some might argue that, from a cultural point of view, the US is somewhat lacking. But what the US brought to the equation for *Doctor Who* is the same thing it often brings to any situation: unbridled enthusiasm. This is not to say that all of America embraced *Doctor Who*. PBS television stations have never been in any sense a mainstream media outlet in the US. Thus the number of viewers exposed to *Doctor Who* was far smaller than the number watching a programme like the comedy-drama *M.A.S.H.* on a national network. But the US has a substantially larger total population than most of the countries in the British Commonwealth, outnumbering the UK itself by nearly four to one in 1980.[78] So, despite the sporadic distribution of *Doctor Who*, the number of people exposed to it was still substantial, even though it was a small percentage of the total population. And, of course, these were American viewers – exuberant,

---

[77] 'Dr Who Takes LA by Storm.' *Starlog*, August 1979, 14. PDF.
[78] 'Data: Population, total.' *The World Bank*, accessed 23 April 2015. http://data.worldbank.org/indicator/SP.POP.TOTL?page=6

unfettered and passionate American viewers.

The impact on *Doctor Who* of this American exposure, and of the subsequent development of an American fan base, was not particularly obvious as the programme entered the 1980s and moved toward its twentieth anniversary. To be sure, a figure adorned in the fourth Doctor's trademark floppy fedora and multicoloured scarf might have been seen occasionally at one of the *Star Trek* fan conventions across the country, and the British import shops might have noted an increase in the popularity of the fourth Doctor's favourite Jelly Babies, but through the early 1980s, *Doctor Who* went mostly unnoticed by the population at large, and the BBC's commercial arm, BBC Enterprises, was content simply to collect periodic modest payments from American distributor Time-Warner.

Despite the modest US success Tom Baker brought to the programme, *Doctor Who* might have just muddled along through the 1970s and into the 1980s, even with some efforts to explore new arenas. In keeping with the long history of science fiction conventions, which expanded notably with the success of *Star Trek*-themed events in the 1970s, *Doctor Who* also became the subject of fan-run events. These started the UK in 1977 with an effort put together by the DWAS. [79] The first US convention, featuring an appearance by Tom Baker, came two years later. [80] These special events, generally held over a particular weekend, were in addition to long-standing permanent BBC Enterprises exhibitions at Blackpool and Longleat, in which fans could see props and exhibits from the programme. While these fan-centred efforts did suggest the potential of *Doctor Who*, they were no more remarkable than similar efforts for other

---

[79] Paul Winter, DWAS, e-mail correspondence with the author, 6 June 2015.
[80] 'Tom Baker: The American Tours.'
thomas-stewart-baker.com, accessed 10 August 2014. http://thomas-stewart-baker.com/americantours.html. While this is a fan site, other dates it gives for Baker's convention appearances are accurate as personally verified by the author, including the memorable Timecon '86, so the 1979 date can be taken as accurate as well.

franchises. The reach of *Doctor Who* in the UK in 1980 was generally comparable to the reach of *Star Trek* in the US at the same time, and both operated far below the vast marketing and merchandising machine that *Star Wars* had become on both sides of the Atlantic.

What happened in 1983 was a game-changer for the programme, and it surpassed all expectations. That year saw the twentieth anniversary of *Doctor Who*. This would be a notable landmark for any television programme, to be certain, and the *Doctor Who* production team prepared a special, feature-length story for the event. This was 'The Five Doctors', featuring then-current Doctor Peter Davison along with Jon Pertwee and Patrick Troughton, Richard Hurndall as a recast first Doctor and a bevy of companions. Outside of the television special, though, 1983 saw *Doctor Who* experience a wave of popularity unlike anything seen since Dalekmania. The exhibitions at Blackpool and Longleat were swarmed with visitors, and a BBC Enterprises-organised convention held over one April weekend at the latter venue was overwhelmed by up to seven times the number of expected attendees.[81] Conventions across the US were mobbed by visitors, kicking off a steady run of annual events, including TARDIS in Chicago, and Timecon in San Jose.[82] 1983 also saw the first *Doctor Who* forays into new areas of media, including video games and home video.

Given the rise of computer technology in the later 1970s and early 1980s, it should be no surprise that *Doctor Who* found itself the subject of a licensed video game. Indeed, the surprise might be that it took as long as it did for a game to be developed. The game itself, *Doctor Who – The First Adventure*, was not especially groundbreaking. It featured play mechanics drawn from other

---

[81] '*Doctor Who* convention.' *TARDIS Data Core*, accessed 10 August 2014. http://tardis.wikia.com/wiki/Doctor_Who_convention

[82] 'Chicago to stage *Doctor Who* convention.' *Television Weekly*, (London, UK) 11 April 1983, page unknown, as found on *Cuttings Archive*, accessed 5 June 2015.
http://cuttingsarchive.org/index.php/Chicago_to_stage_Dr_Who_convention

popular games of the time, such as *Frogger* and *Pac-Man*, and offered graphics on par with other 8-bit titles of the era, which is to say that it featured chunky sprites that required a great deal of imagination to invest in.[83] But, for the first time, a player could electronically become the Doctor, and battle alien foes digitally. The game was a modest success, but served as a reminder that mediocre game play with a big media name attached was not a guarantee of sales or popularity; a fact that BBC Enterprises could have gleaned from a spectacular demonstration by Atari with its colossal 1982 video-game flop based on the film *E.T. The Extra-Terrestrial*. However, the video game was only one part of BBC Enterprises' plans to expand *Doctor Who* into new media.

The twentieth anniversary year also saw the very first release of *Doctor Who* in another new media format, that of home video. Based on a survey taken at the huge Longleat convention in April 1983, the BBC Video division of BBC Enterprises put out the Tom Baker story 'Revenge of the Cybermen' as its first VHS tape featuring the Doctor.[84] As a nod to the demonstrable fan base in North America, the video was released both in the PAL format for British purchasers, and in the NTSC format for those in the US and Canada. By 1983, home video was not especially new, as the first video cassette player, the Betamax SL-6300, had been announced by Sony in

---

[83] *Radio Times Doctor Who 20th Anniversary Special.* (London: *Radio Times*, 1983), p 41.
[84] 'BBC release drama, LE on cassette.' *The Stage and Television Today*, (London, UK) 15 September 1983. p 15. A *Doctor Who* wiki source notes that 'The Tomb of the Cybermen' was actually the preferred choice by fans. Independent verification of this data is not readily available, but most fans do seem to have long memories. It is believed that many fans completing the survey wrote 'The Tomb of the Cybermen' as a joke, knowing that that it was missing from the archives at the time, and BBC Video assumed that any Cyberman story would be equally well received.

1975.[85] But by the early 1980s, the video market had reached a sort of critical mass, where the new video-rental shops provided viewers a greater degree of control over their viewing habits than they had ever had before. Drawing on the earlier legacy of viewers making audio recordings of favourite stories, the BBC rightly assumed that there would be a ready market for videocassettes of *Doctor Who* serials. The programme would continue to have a notable presence in that market during the 1980s, although it was nothing like the near-instantaneous distribution it enjoys in the 21st Century.

Alas, 1983 arguably marked a high point for the classic programme. The rest of the 1980s was a difficult time for *Doctor Who*, and for *Doctor Who* fans. Despite John Nathan-Turner's efforts to update the production to a more contemporary style, viewing figures were slipping. The budget was still relatively low, and money tended to run out, so that by the end of production on a given season, the monsters might be little more than cobbled-together bits of fluff and foam. It didn't help that a number of BBC executives, including the then Controller of BBC One Michael Grade, seem to have had almost a vendetta against *Doctor Who*. As a result, the programme went through a series of arguably damaging changes during the mid-1980s. The first of these was a format change for Season Twenty-Two from 25-minute episodes to 45-minute episodes, with a corresponding reduction in the number of episodes produced per season, making for a difficult start for Colin Baker's Doctor, already hampered with a tailor's nightmare of an outfit. Then Grade and his colleagues decided to suspend production on *Doctor Who* for a year, creating an 18-month gap between seasons rather than that usual six-month gap, theoretically to allow it to retool for less violence and better writing. This made a positive perception of Baker's Doctor even more difficult, especially because when he returned for Season Twenty-Three, the

---

[85] 'Chapter1 [sic] The Video Cassette Tape.' *Sony*, accessed 8 May 2015. http://www.sony.net/SonyInfo/CorporateInfo/History/SonyHistory/2-01.html

episode count was only 14, but the episode length had returned to the original 25-minute format.

After the 18-month wait, the programme's fans tuned in with a mix of eagerness and apprehension. Despite the blurry opening titles and questionably disco-ised theme music, when they saw the opening shots of the first episode of the story called 'The Trial of a Time Lord', there was a collective gasp at what was, compared to previous seasons, a really remarkably good effects shot of the TARDIS being sucked into a giant spacecraft. It appeared, at least at the start of episode one, that this might well be a new *Doctor Who* after all. By the end of the fourteenth and last episode, it was clear this was not the case. The season had been troubled by behind-the-scenes problems with both writing and script editing. Companion Peri had been written out almost as perfunctorily as Dodo had been in the 1960s. The conclusion of the overall story arc was equally murky, the product of last-minute changes and rewriting that left Baker little to work with. To make matters worse, the BBC executives subsequently instructed Nathan-Turner to fire the actor.

Sylvester McCoy stepped in to bring the Doctor up to date, accompanied by a flashy set of CGI titles and an effort to adhere to higher productions values. Admittedly, McCoy brought a striking depth to his version of the Doctor. His performance also offered hints of the darker undercurrents that are so prominent in the revived programme. While sixth Doctor holdover companion Mel was not terribly well received, McCoy's repartee with Sophie Aldred as rough-and-tumble newcomer Ace also seemed to fit well with the mood of the late 1980s, and it seemed possible *Doctor Who* might have a new lease of life, although the twenty-fifth anniversary celebration was much more muted than the twentieth had been. Alas, it was not to be, and 1989 saw the conclusion of the initial run of *Doctor Who*.

There it might have ended, were it not for a fundamental shift taking place in the way society consumed media. Had *Doctor Who* been cancelled in the 1960s or 1970s, it is unlikely it would have had much of an enduring presence. Once a programme was off the air, it was finished, unless some smaller television station opted to pick up syndicated episodes. However, *Doctor Who* did endure, because by 1989, the home video market had matured. People had rapidly accepted the idea of viewing both films and television programmes at home on a videocassette unit, with the ability to pause, rewind and rewatch happily. The cost of videocassettes had dropped dramatically, and availability had exploded, leaving videotapes available almost everywhere, including the local grocer's shop and even petrol stations. Wisely, BBC Video had capitalised on this trend. The single video release of *Doctor Who* in 1983 had become a steady stream of titles by 1989, including stories featuring all of the first five Doctors. These tapes were released both in the UK and overseas. The rate at which new videos were released actually increased after the final series of *Doctor Who* was broadcast in 1989. In the early 1990s, there was clearly a strong market for *Doctor Who* on videotape; strong enough that BBC Video even began to release tapes featuring individual episodes from incomplete stories that has been purged during the 1970s.

There is an interesting question to consider regarding the release of those partial stories and orphaned episodes. It is one thing to want to have a copy of a favourite story or series from a television programme. However, it is something else entirely to have a large enough group of people willing to pay for their own copy of something that is not only incomplete, but almost certain to remain that way. When viewers sat down to watch episode two of 'The Abominable Snowmen', released in 1991 as part of *The Troughton Years* video, they knew that they would not be able to see episode three, probably ever. Yet enough people watched the tapes to prompt further releases of incomplete stories, sometimes using one of the original actors to fill in with connecting narration, as on the initial release of the Patrick Troughton serial 'The Invasion' and the unfinished Tom Baker serial 'Shada'. It is difficult to state definitively why such partial stories were successful sellers, but one general sentiment among fans of the programme was that they represented crucial elements of the past for *Doctor Who*, and that being able to see and hear a Yeti, or watch the Cybermen walk down the steps of St Paul's Cathedral, was a way to understand better the programme they enjoyed so much. Such an attitude is quite telling, as few programmes inspire such a devoted following.

One might wonder, given the success of the video releases, why the programme no longer ran on BBC television. If the brand was so popular, why not bring it back after another 'hiatus'? Plans were, in fact, under way for such a revival, but it was here that the American fan base proved a decisive factor, both for good and for ill. When *Doctor Who* finally did return to television in 1996, it was in America, as a joint American and British production. Studio executives were convinced there was enough of an American audience to bring the Doctor back, in part perhaps due to the success of fan-run *Doctor Who* conventions such as Gallifrey One in Los Angeles, which at the time of writing is planning for its twenty-seventh annual event. The fact that these conventions were so well attended, despite the lack of new stories for several years, meant there had to be a market for *Doctor Who*. Rather than attempt to reboot the programme, the 1996 TV movie acknowledged it was a continuation of what had gone before, even giving Sylvester McCoy a send-off and regeneration scene in the first few minutes of the action before Paul McGann stepped in to become the Doctor.

However, McCoy and McGann were the only British elements evident on screen. Otherwise the story was an entirely American-style one, complete with random gang violence to prompt a regeneration sequence, sleazy hospital executives, an over-the-top incarnation of the Master and a muddled conclusion to a ponderous storyline. While not an abject failure, neither was it a marked success, and it seemed a television revival of *Doctor Who* was not to be.

If *Doctor Who* was effectively dead on television, the body had certainly not stopped moving. In 1991, Virgin began publishing a series of New Adventures, with stories featuring the seventh Doctor and Ace, and later introducing other new companions.[86] 1993 then saw *Doctor Who* return to television, albeit only briefly, as a special thirtieth anniversary short was created featuring all the living Doctors for the annual *Children in Need* telethon. Starting in 1998, Big Finish began producing *Doctor Who*-related audio dramas, including both New Adventures adaptations and original stories.[87] These original stories gave Paul McGann's Doctor a whole new lease on life, as well as providing avenues for other classic-series Doctors to engage in exciting new adventures.

In addition, there were continued efforts to recover missing stories, including efforts to find or recreate colour versions of some Jon Pertwee-era stories of which only black and white copies remained in the archives at that time. Using a variety of methods to extract or overlay colour data, stories such 'The Daemons' and 'Doctor Who and the Silurians' were restored to colour, even if the clarity was not quite as good as it had been originally, due to incompatibilities between British and American broadcast formats, as well as slight image distortions introduced during the making of film transfers. Such meticulous and expensive efforts speak both to the success of *Doctor Who* and to the potential it has for exploring both the technical and the social frontiers of diverse aspects of media.

If there was any doubt that *Doctor Who* was a suitable vehicle to explore media for the masses, BBC Video surely set this to rest in 1999 when the twentieth anniversary story 'The Five Doctors' was one of the first DVDs put out as a test of the

---

[86] 'Virgin New Adventures.' *TARDIS Data Core*, accessed 2 May 2015. http://tardis.wikia.com/wiki/Virgin_New_Adventures. Virgin no longer makes the New Adventures books, and so no data is currently available for the early releases on their web site.

[87] Gary Russell. 'The Frequently Asked Questions List.' *Big Finish*, 2002, as found on *webarchive.org*, accessed 2 May 2015. http://web.archive.org/web/20021016233937/http://www.doctorwho.co.uk/faq.htm

market for this new format.[88] The DVD market proved to be, if anything, even more successful than the VHS one had been, and a veritable torrent of *Doctor Who* DVDs issued forth from the BBC vaults during the first decade of the 21st Century. Noteworthy releases included the *Lost in Time* compilation of episodes from missing stories, and a fresh approach to restoring a fragmentary story, wherein computer animation was used to reconstruct two missing episodes of 'The Invasion'. This method of restoration was not cheap, resulting in an expensive DVD release, but it again demonstrates the significance of *Doctor Who* as a media icon that BBC Video was willing to undertake such an effort.

As the DVD releases gathered momentum, *Doctor Who* finally did return to BBC television in 2005 with the launch of the revived programme. The history of the work that went into the revival has been well-discussed elsewhere, including in J Shaun Lyon's book *Back to the Vortex* (Telos Publishing, 2005). This revived programme was a whole new kind of *Doctor Who*, with a budget and production values much higher than during the classic era. Most prominently, though, from the start, the revived *Doctor Who* tapped into the global media system with which the BBC was intimately connected.

Doctor Who was everywhere in 2005, and almost as fast as a new outlet opened, it found a presence there. A DVD set of the entire first series was announced very quickly, of course. Video clips of the new programme began appearing on the internet. *Doctor Who* popped up regularly on the various social networking outlets as they grew and developed. The marketing machine ramped up as the revived series progressed, and soon *Doctor Who* was on everything from coffee mugs to T-shirts to mobile phone cases. Soundtrack albums came out regularly, and fan-edited videos permeated on YouTube and other video

---

[88] 'List of BBC DVD Releases.' *TARDIS Data Core,* accessed 10 August 2014. http://tardis.wikia.com/wiki/List_of_BBC_DVD_releases. This release is no longer available on the BBC's catalogue, but copies are available through online sources such as eBay and Amazon.

sites. New finds of previously missing episodes from 1960s stories, such as 'The Web of Fear', became media events in their own right.

A climax to the new media machine that was *Doctor Who* came on 23 November 2013. The fiftieth anniversary story, 'The Day of the Doctor', demonstrated more than any other *Doctor Who*-centred event just how extensive the media penetration of the programme had become, and how profoundly society was willing to embrace this new media. The feature-length story was shown literally across the globe, both on televisions and in cinemas, in the largest simulcast in history.[89] Within minutes of its broadcast, social media sites such as Facebook and Twitter were flooded with commentary, feedback and discussion, leading some to complain about 'spoilers' if they had been unable to catch the simulcast or had to time-shift it by recording. Most meaningfully, a far larger segment of society than had ever been engaged with the programme before now embraced and accepted every facet they could of the media presence of *Doctor Who*. For many fans, no longer was it enough simply to watch the programme. Now a Whovian wearing a *Doctor Who* dressing gown and *Doctor Who* socks can sip tea from a *Doctor Who* mug while viewing *Doctor Who* videos on a tablet and chatting to a *Doctor Who* website using a phone that makes *Doctor Who* sound effects for a ringtone and is wrapped in a *Doctor Who* case.

If there were any lingering doubt that *Doctor Who* represented a new frontier in the way society and media interacted, consider the way the current Doctor, played by Peter Capaldi, was introduced and promoted. Once Matt Smith announced he was leaving the programme, speculation ran rampant on who would step into the TARDIS to replace him. As was not uncommon for previous regenerations, several

---

[89] John Bowman. 'Anniversary episode awarded Guinness World Record.' *Doctor Who News*, 24 November 2013, accessed 17 June 2015. http://www.doctorwhonews.net/2013/11/anniversary-episode-guinness-world-record-241113170417.html

sources ran different odds on a suite of actors likely being considered for the job. But the moment of the great reveal was something quite new, as the BBC hosted a live television special in which previous actors who had been the Doctor weighed in and gave advice to the new prospect before Capaldi strode onto stage to stake his claim to the TARDIS. Admittedly it was not great viewing, but the effort to put together a live television programme simply to talk about another television programme is noteworthy at least. Then, as the premiere of Series Eight neared, Peter Capaldi and co-star Jenna Coleman, the actress who played companion Clara Oswald, embarked on a worldwide tour that saw masses of people turn out to greet them in a spectacle not entirely unlike the Beatlemania images from the 1960s.

Doctor Who has clearly come a very long way from its humble beginnings as a media device. At the same time, it has always been a way to explore just how far the populace will engage with the media. The Dalek toys and audio recordings of the 1960s were exciting, and spoke to the potential of *Doctor Who* as a phenomenon. That potential does indeed seem to have been fulfilled in 2015, as the reach of the programme from the television into audio, print, merchandise, video, conventions and cyberspace rivals any other media entity one could name. The programme has served as an effective way for the public as a whole to explore and get comfortable with new media, just as it has allowed viewers to ponder new ideas of science, technology and society.

Conclusion

Doctor Who is a remarkable programme. That much should be clear. *Doctor Who* is also a unique programme, standing alone as the longest-running science-fiction television drama in history. From its modest if promising beginnings, it has gone on to become a global media empire, providing its viewers with a powerful lens by which the past fifty years can be evaluated.

In light of the seemingly unstoppable media tidal wave *Doctor Who* seems to be riding today, one might ask whether or not it is the same programme it has always been. The answer must be a guarded yes, with some notable conditions. While it set out to be a family programme, one of the aims of which was to help young viewers key in to science and history, the arrival of the Daleks occasioned a paradigm shift that quickly moved it in a different direction. The Daleks also prompted a crashing wave of media hype, at least within the limits of what the 1960s could offer. Granted, for much of the classic programme's run, the special effects were limited; but, for the most part, the stories were good. The special effects are more polished now, the production values are higher, but at its heart, good stories are what make *Doctor Who* work, not flashy visuals.

It is in those stories that *Doctor Who* has provided a safety valve for society as a whole to evaluate many facets of itself. When computers were new and perhaps threatening, *Doctor Who* offered viewers several 'what if?' scenarios to consider, until such technology became ubiquitous and stopped being quite so suitable as science fiction fodder. When medicine seemed to be on the verge of untold new possibilities, *Doctor Who* served as a way to evaluate the unintended consequences of those possibilities; and when the prospects for various

CONCLUSION

physical and virtual immortalities presented themselves, again, *Doctor Who* provided a safe way to think those ideas through. When gender roles were in flux, and when complex moral problems asserted themselves, *Doctor Who* was there to help matters along with its own particular kind of wisdom, allowing society to agree or disagree as necessary.

Doctor Who is a mirror of ourselves and our world. The world of the 1960s was not as media-savvy or technologically capable as the world of the 21st Century, but the programme still served then the same principal function as it does today. *Doctor Who* offers a means to explore a constantly evolving, increasingly globalised and strikingly technological world. When the Doctor steps up to defeat the Daleks, the Cybermen or the Weeping Angels, we see in his actions an affirmation of our own efforts to navigate successfully through and cope with the rapid and sometimes terrifying changes all around us. As valuable as *Doctor Who* is in the context of social history, it is vital to recall its primary function. *Doctor Who* is, and always has been, an incredible and enjoyable escape from the concerns and problems of reality, when it threatens to become overwhelming and we just need a little break to watch a madman in a box make everything right with the world again.

Bibliography

'1956: Queen switches on nuclear power.' BBC News, 2007, accessed 23 February 2014.
http://news.bbc.co.uk/onthisday/hi/dates/stories/october/17/newsid_3147000/3147145.stm

'1966: BBC tunes in to colour.' BBC News, 2008, accessed 23 April 2015.
http://news.bbc.co.uk/onthisday/hi/dates/stories/march/3/newsid_2514000/2514719.stm

'A Short History of Radio.' FCC, winter 2003, accessed 21 January 2014.
http://transition.fcc.gov/omd/history/radio/documents/short_history.pdf

'A Timeline of AIDS.' AIDS.gov, accessed 8 January 2014.
http://aids.gov/hiv-aids-basics/hiv-aids-101/aids-timeline/

'Apollo Flight Tests' NASA, 1968, accessed 24 March 2014.
http://www.hq.nasa.gov/alsj/CSM05_Apollo_Flt_Tests_pp33-38.pdf pp. 33-38.

'At DARPA Challenge, Robots (Slowly) Move Toward Better Disaster Recovery.' NPR, 7 June 2015, accessed 10 June 2015.
http://www.npr.org/sections/alltechconsidered/2015/06/07/412533020/at-darpa-challenge-robots-slowly-move-toward-better-disaster-recovery

'BBC release drama, LE on cassette.' *The Stage and Television Today*, (London, UK) 15 September 1983. p 15.

BIBLIOGRAPHY

'Biography of Mary Quant.' Victoria and Albert Museum, 2015, accessed 9 June 2015.
http://www.vam.ac.uk/content/articles/m/mary-quant/

'Breaking the Code.' Computer History Museum. 2015, accessed 5 April 2015.
http://www.computerhistory.org/revolution/birth-of-the-computer/4/82

'By the Numbers: Worldwide Deaths.' National WWII Museum, accessed 12 March 2014.
http://www.nationalww2museum.org/learn/education/for-students/ww2-history/ww2-by-the-numbers/world-wide-deaths.html

'Celestial Archive.' *Doctor Who* Appreciation Society, accessed 9 August 2014.
http://www.dwasonline.co.uk/celestial_archive

'Chapter1 [sic] The Video Cassette Tape.' Sony, accessed 8 May 2015.
http://www.sony.net/SonyInfo/CorporateInfo/History/SonyHistory/2-01.html

'Chicago to stage *Doctor Who* convention.' *Television Weekly*, (London, UK) 11 April 1983, page unknown, as found on Cuttings Archive, accessed 5 June 2015.
http://cuttingsarchive.org/index.php/Chicago_to_stage_Dr_Who_convention

'Cooperation for Recovery: The Marshall Plan' International Monetary Fund, accessed 12 March 2014.
http://www.imf.org/external/np/exr/center/mm/eng/mm_dr_03.htm

'Dalek Toy History.' doctorwhotoys.net accessed 23 July 2014.
http://www.doctorwhotoys.net/dalektoyhistory.htm

'Data: Population, total.' The World Bank, accessed 23 April 2015.
http://data.worldbank.org/indicator/SP.POP.TOTL?page=6

'*Doctor Who* convention.' TARDIS Data Core, accessed 10 August 2014.
http://tardis.wikia.com/wiki/Doctor_Who_convention

'*Doctor Who Magazine* wins Guinness World Record.' Doctor Who News, 1 October 2010, accessed 9 August 2014.
http://www.doctorwhonews.net/2010/04/doctor-who-magazine-wins-guinness-world.html

'Dr Who's sonic screwdriver "invented" at Dundee University.' BBC News, 19 April 2012, accessed 9 March 2014.
http://www.bbc.com/news/uk-scotland-17760077

'Dr Who Takes LA by Storm.' *Starlog*, August 1979, 14. PDF.

'Early Colour Television.' Early Television Museum, accessed 12 February 2014.
http://www.earlytelevision.org/british_ntsc_color.html

'Google's street-level maps raising concerns.' USA Today, 1 June 2007, accessed 31 December 2013.
http://usatoday30.usatoday.com/tech/news/internetprivacy/2007-06-01-google-maps-privacy_N.htm

'History of the BBC.' BBC, accessed 22 January 2014.
http://www.bbc.co.uk/historyofthebbc/resources/factsheets/1920s.pdf

BIBLIOGRAPHY

'List of BBC DVD Releases.' TARDIS Data Core, accessed 10 August 2014.
http://tardis.wikia.com/wiki/List_of_BBC_DVD_releases

'Long Runners.' TVTropes.org. Accessed 1 December 2013.
http://tvtropes.org/pmwiki/pmwiki.php/Main/LongRunners

'Mariner 1.' NASA, 2014, accessed 28 November 2013.
http://nssdc.gsfc.nasa.gov/nmc/spacecraftDisplay.do?id=MARIN1

'Median and Average Sales Prices of New Homes Sold in the US.' US Census Bureau, accessed 2 January 2014.
http://www.census.gov/const/uspriceann.pdf

'Milestones in Organ Transplantation.' National Kidney Foundation, 2015, accessed 14 April 2015.
https://www.kidney.org/transplantation/transaction/Milestones-Organ-Transplantation

'Nova/Super Nova' sales brochure. Southborough: Data General, ND, before 1970. PDF as found at Computer History Museum, accessed 2 January 2014.
http://www.computerhistory.org/brochures/companies.php?alpha=d-f#

'Radio Shack TRS 80 (Model 1).' oldcomputers.net, 10 December 2013, accessed 2 January 2014.
http://oldcomputers.net/trs80i.html

'Rise of the Cybermen (TV story)' TARDIS Data Core, accessed 8 January 2014,
 tardis.wikia.com/wiki/Rise_of_the_Cybermen_(TV_story)

'Samuel F B Morse Sent the First Telegraphic Message May 24 1844.' America's Library, accessed 12 February 2014.
http://www.americaslibrary.gov/jb/reform/jb_reform_morse cod_1.html

'Sinclair ZX80.' oldcomputers.net, 10 December 2013, accessed 2 January 2014.
http://oldcomputers.net/trs80i.html

'Strategic Arms Limitations Talks (SALT 1).' US State Department, accessed 14 March 2014.
http://www.state.gov/www/global/arms/treaties/salt1.html

'Target Books.' TARDIS Data Core, accessed 9 August 2014.
http://tardis.wikia.com/wiki/Target_Books

'Television ownership in private domestic households 1956-2014 (millions)' Broadcast Audience Research Board, accessed 23 April 2015.
http://www.barb.co.uk/resources/tv-facts/tv-ownership

'The Battle of Gettysburg: Statistics.' US Army, accessed 12 March 2014.
http://www.army.mil/gettysburg/statistics/statistics.html

'Timeline of Computer History: 1941.' Computer History Museum, 2006, accessed 26 November 2013.
computerhistory.org/timeline/year=1941

'Timeline of Computer History: 1968.' Computer History Museum, 2006, accessed 2 January 2014.
computerhistory.org/timeline/year=1968?

'Timeline of Computer History: 1972.' Computer History Museum, 2006, accessed 2 January 2014.
computerhistory.org/timeline/year=1972

BIBLIOGRAPHY

'Timeline of Computer History: 1974.' Computer History Museum, 2006, accessed 3 January 2014.
computerhistory.org/timeline/year=1974

'Tom Baker: The American Tours.' thomas-stewart-baker.com, accessed 10 August 2014.
http://thomas-stewart-baker.com/americantours.html.

'Virgin New Adventures.' TARDIS Data Core, accessed 2 May 2015. http://tardis.wikia.com/wiki/Virgin_New_Adventures.

'ZX81: Small black box of computing desire.' BBC News, 11 March, 2011, accessed 2 January 2014.
http://www.bbc.co.uk/news/magazine-12703674

Advertisements section. *The Strand Magazine*, November 1892. i-xii.

Asaro, Peter. 'Heinz Von Foerster and the Bio-Computing Movements of the 1960s' in *An Unfinished Revolution: Heinz Von Foerster and the Biological Computer Laboratory*, BCL, 1958-1976, ed. Albert Müller, Karl H Müller. (Edition Echoraum, 2007), 257-259. PDF at
http://www.stim.illinois.edu/unfinishedrev/11_asaro.pdf ----- totl pp(255-275)

Banks, David. *Doctor Who: Cybermen*. London: W H Allen & Co, 1990.

BBC Annual Report and Accounts 2013/2014. London: British Broadcasting Corporation, 2014,
PDF.

BBC Worldwide Annual Review 2012-2013. Kent: Cousin, 2013,
PDF.

Bowman, John. 'Anniversary episode awarded Guinness World Record.' Doctor Who News, 24 November 2013, accessed 17 June 2015.
http://www.doctorwhonews.net/2013/11/anniversary-episode-guinness-world-record-241113170417.html

Copeland, Jack. 'Colossus: The First Large Scale Electronic Computer.' colosuss-computer.com, 2001, accessed 5 April 2015.
http://www.colossus-computer.com/index.htm

Deal, Ryan. 'Hottest Gadgets of the 1960s.' Techvert, 18 June 2010, accessed 13 January 2014.
http://www.techvert.com/gadgets-of-the-1960s/

Foster, Chuck. 'Missing Radio Script Discovered.' Doctor Who News, 15 January 2012, accessed 23 April 2015.
http://www.doctorwhonews.net/2012/01/dwn150112121012-missing-radio-script.html

Gorney, Cynthia. 'Dr Seuss at 75: Grinch, Cat in Hat, Wocket and Generations of Kids in His Pocket'. *The Washington Post* (Washington, DC) 21 May 1979.

Grossman, Samantha. '1 in 4 Americans Apparently Unaware the Earth Orbits the Sun' *Time*, 16 February 2014, accessed 19 April 2015.
http://time.com/7809/1-in-4-americans-thinks-sun-orbits-earth/

Jackson, Harold. 'The Curse of the Daleks at Wyndham's.' *Guardian*. 22 December 1965, page unknown, as found at Cuttings Archive, accessed 1 May 2015.
http://cuttingsarchive.org/index.php/The_Curse_of_the_Daleks_at_Wyndham%27s

BIBLIOGRAPHY

Jenkins, Alan. 'For 14 years now, a science fiction program, *Doctor Who* has been frightening and entertaining children in Britain.' *The Palm Beach Post* (Palm Beach, FL), 26 August 1978, TV1-2. PDF.

Kahn, Jordan. 'Five years after launch: Apple sold 250M iPhones, accounting for $150B in revenue.' *9to5 Mac*, 27 June 2012, accessed 5 March 2014.
http://9to5mac.com/2012/06/27/5-years-after-launch-apple-has-sold-250-million-iphones-accounting-for-150b-in-revenue/

Kay, Susan. 'Why Can't They Write for Women?' *The Stage and Television Today*. (London) 19 November 1964.

Keegn, John. *The First World War*. New York: Vintage, 1998.

Letter, Soviet Premier Nikita Khrushchev to President Kennedy, 26 October 1962 as reproduced in *Major Problems in American History Since 1945*. (Boston: Wadsworth), 2007, 144-147.

Locker, Melissa. 'Scientists Finally Invent Real, Working Lightsabers.' *Time*, 1 October 2013, accessed 9 March 2014.
http://newsfeed.time.com/2013/10/01/someone-finally-invented-real-working-lightsabers/

Mailer, John S and Barbara Mason. 'Penicillin: Medicine's Wartime Wonder Drug and Its Production at Peoria, Illinois.' Northern Illinois University, accessed 5 January 2014.
http://www.lib.niu.edu/2001/iht810139.html

Mandel, Ananya, MD. 'Hip Replacement History' News Medical, 16 October 2014, accessed 6 January 2015.
http://www.news-medical.net/health/Hip-Replacement-History.aspx

Movietone News [undated, circa 1946]. Directed by Edmund Reek. 20th Century Fox, 1946. YouTube video http://m.youtube.com/watch?v=OSYpYFEwr4o accessed 2 September 2014

Newman, Sydney, Memo to Carole Ann Ford, 28 October 1964 as found on 'Moments in Time – Goodbye Susan, Goodbye My Dear.' Doctor Who News, 26 December 2014, accessed 27 December 2014.
http://www.doctorwhonews.net/2014/12/moments-in-time-goodbye-susan-goodbye.html

Norris, Marjorie. 'Meant for children but this will get a much wider audience.' *The Stage and Television Today.* (London) 5 December 1963, as found on
http://cuttingsarchive.org/images/a/a5/1963-12-05_Stage_and_Television_Today.jpg

Radio Times Doctor Who 20th Anniversary Special. (London: Radio Times, 1983), p 41.

Russell, Gary. 'The Frequently Asked Questions List.' Big Finish, 2002, as found on webarchive.org, accessed 2 May 2015. http://web.archive.org/web/20021016233937/http://www.doctorwho.co.uk/faq.htm

Sandeep, Jauhar, MD, PhD. 'The Artificial Heart.' *New England Journal of Medicine* (2004): 542-544.

Solanis, Valerie. 'The SCUM Manifesto.' Womynkind.org, accessed 29 April 2014.
http://www.womynkind.org/scum.htm

The Machine that Changed the World: 'Giant Brains.' Directed by John Palfreman. PBS, 1992. YouTube video
https://www.youtube.com/watch?v=kYFRdV1r4nU.

BIBLIOGRAPHY

The Machine That Changed the World: 'Inventing the Future.' Directed by John Palfreman. PBS, 1992. YouTube video https://www.youtube.com/watch?v=GropWVbj9wA

Weik, Mark. 'The ENIAC Story.' *Ordnance*, January-February 1961 as reproduced at http://ftp.arl.mil/mike/comphist/eniac-story.html accessed 2 September 2014.

Whitaker, David. *Doctor Who and the Daleks*. (UK: BBC Books/Random House, 1964, 2011), 1-16.

White, Thomas H. 'Broadcasting After World War I (1918-1921).' earlyradiohistory.us, accessed 22 January 2016. http://earlyradiohistory.us/sec016.htm

White, Thomas H. 'Big Business and Radio (1915 - 1922).' earlyradiohistory.us, accessed 22 January 2014. http://earlyradiohistory.us/sec017.htm

Zimmerman, Kim Ann. 'Internet History Timeline: From ARPANET to the World Wide Web'. *Live Science*. 4 June 2012, accessed 14 January, 2016.
http://www.livescience.com/20727-internet-history.html

About the Author

David Johnson MA is Professor of History for Colorado Northwestern Community College in Colorado, USA. His field of study is modern European history, with a preference for British history. He has a previously published essay in the book *Time and Relative Dimensions in Faith: Religion and Doctor Who* (Darton, Longman & Todd, 2013) and has been a fan of the programme since the mid-1980s, when he discovered it as a teenager. He was actively involved with *Doctor Who* fandom for many years, including assisting with the first two Gallifrey One conventions in Los Angeles.

www.ingramcontent.com/pod-product-compliance
Lightning Source LLC
Chambersburg PA
CBHW071346080526
44587CB00017B/2989